The Battle of Wakefield Revisited:

A Fresh Perspective on Richard of York's Final Battle, December 1460

Helen Cox

Published by Helen Cox
Herstory Writing & Interpretation
www.helencox-herstorywriting.co.uk

First published in 2010 by
Herstory Writing & Interpretation/York Publishing Services
R.R.P. £12.00

ISBN 978-0-9565768-0-4

Cover illustration: The death of Richard, Duke of York – detail from polychrome
plaster frieze in Wakefield County Hall.

Typeset and printed by:

York Publishing Services,
64, Hallfield Road,
Layerthorpe,
York YO31 7ZQ
Telephone enquiries: 01904 431213
Email enquiries: enqs@yps-publishing.co.uk
Website: www.yps-publishing.co.uk

Order from: www.YPD-books.com

CONTENTS

A Note on the Author

Originally qualified as an archaeological conservator, Helen Cox spent 15 years working in museums in Britain and the United States before specialising as a freelance heritage consultant. In 2005, she took early retirement to pursue long-held research interests in medieval history, becoming an active member of the Richard III Society and Towton Battlefield Society. Now based in Wakefield, Helen works as a freelance writer, lecturer and Wars of the Roses interpreter. Recent publications include articles for the *Ricardian Bulletin* and *The Yorkshire Dalesman*, and a chapter in the second edition of the Battle of Towton excavation report, *Blood Red Roses*. She also edits *The Towton Herald*, newsletter of Towton Battlefield Society, and is Secretary of the Society's affiliated Wars of the Roses re-enactment group, The Frei Compagnie.

List of Illustrations

Unless otherwise stated, all photographs and line drawings are by the author.

Plate 1: The drum towers and sally-port at Sandal Castle.
Plate 2: Detail of polychrome plaster frieze in Wakefield County Hall.
Plate 3: Princess Margaret of Anjou.
Plate 4: Queen Margaret at prayer from a Skinners' Company manuscript held at the Guildhall, City of London. Photo by Ted Hall; reproduced by kind permission of The Skinners' Company.
Plate 5: Detail from the 'Neville Window' at St Andrew's Church, Penrith. Photo by Alistair Harper.
Plate 6: Stained glass window from Trinity College Library, showing Richard of York in armour. Photo by Les Goodey; reproduced by kind permission of the Master and Fellows of Trinity College, Cambridge.
Plate 7: Ridge-and-furrow in Castle Grove Park, near the site of York's fall.
Plate 8: Detail of 1610 map showing the deer-parks at Wakefield and Sandal. Photo by Sally Mills; reproduced by kind permission of West Yorkshire Archive Service, Wakefield, ref. C559/76.
Plate 9: Sandal Castle, 1562, drawn from 'Duchy of Lancaster Maps and Plans 1562 – 4', The National Archives, MPC 1/97.
Plate 10: Environs of Sandal Castle showing the conjectured positions of the deer-park and Yorkist camp. Photo by Roger Keech, © RK Stills 2007.
Plate 11: Portobello spearhead; reproduced by kind permission of Wakefield Council.
Plate 12: The chantry chapel on Wakefield's medieval bridge.
Plate 13: Speed's 1610 map showing Wakefield and its environs. Photo by Sally Mills; reproduced by kind permission of West Yorkshire Archive Service, Wakefield, ref. C559/76.
Plate 14: The Duke of York's monument c. 1900 by Eric Raper, reproduced by kind permission of the Raper family and the online archive of Wakefield District images, www.twixtaireandcalder.org.uk.
Plate 15: Aerial view of Sandal Castle and the battlefield. Photo by Roger Keech, © RK Stills 2007.
Plate 16: Lord Dacre's tomb in Saxton churchyard.

Figure 1: Map showing known or conjectured troop movements in December 1460.
Figure 2: Feature map of Wakefield.
Figure 3: Conjectured troop deployment at the start of the battle.
Figure 4: Conjectured early battle manoeuvres.
Figure 5: The 'environing'.

Acknowledgements

A great many individuals and organisations have helped bring this book to fruition. Among them, special thanks must go to:

- Towton Battlefield Society, especially the Chairman, Mark Taylor, and Secretary, Graham Darbyshire, for supplying background information; to archaeologist Paul Bennett, for technical help with Chapter 6; and to Roger Keech for generously allowing me to use his aerial photographs.
- The Richard III Society, particularly Peter Hammond for greatly improving the draft text with constructive criticism; Lesley Boatwright for invaluable help with Latin translations; and Dr. John Ashdown-Hill for information on medieval seals.
- Wakefield Libraries, especially Jean Atkinson at Kettlethorpe Branch Library, and Deborah Scriven, Library Area Supervisor, for their diligent work in pursuing my many requests.
- West Yorkshire Archive Service, Wakefield Headquarters, particularly Senior Archivist Catherine Taylor; Archivists Gary Brannan and Geoff Brown; and Archive Assistants Sally Mills and Andrew Young, for all their help with my frequent enquiries.
- Staff of the Reading Room, British Library, Boston Spa.
- Staff at Wakefield Museum, particularly Pamela Judkins, Senior Officer, Collections Management.
- Authors Annette Carson, David Cooke and Richard Moore for supplying information and encouragement.

For help with various aspects of my research, I am also greatly indebted to:

Virginia Baddeley, Sites and Monuments Record Officer, Nottinghamshire County Council; Mervyn Bassett and Ted Hall, The Skinners' Company; Anthea Boylston, University of Bradford; Ian Brandt; Sophie Burton, English Heritage/National Monuments Record; Professor Richard Gameson, University of Durham; Samantha Glasswell, Curator, Bassetlaw Museum; Jeremy Godwin; Andrew Gray, Archivist, Durham University Library; Allan Harley; Alistair Harper; Stuart Ivinson, Librarian, Royal Armouries; Dr. Kevin Leahy; Peter Lester, Archivist, Nottinghamshire Archives; Adrian Norris; David Rayner; Ian Roberts, Principal Archaeologist, West Yorkshire Archaeology Service; James Robinson and Naomi Speakman, British Museum; Tom Robson, Senior Archivist, Cumbria Archive Service; Dr. James Ross, The National Archives; Gabriel Sewell, Lambeth Palace Library; Jonathan Smith, Trinity College Library; Joan Williams,

Durham Cathedral Library; Robert Yorke, Archivist, College of Arms; Yorkshire Archaeological Society.

Last but not least I would like to thank my husband, Mick Doggett, who introduced me to Sandal Castle and the catastrophe that took place on its doorstep, and spent countless hours tramping the sites and commenting on the work in progress. Without his unstinting encouragement and support, this book would never have been written.

Helen Cox
March 2010

Plate 1: Sandal Castle, one of the Duke of York's residences: the drum towers at the base of the keep staircase, with the sally-port doorway in the background.

INTRODUCTION

Many people associate the name of Richard, Duke of York, with a derisive nursery rhyme, a mnemonic for the colours of the rainbow (Richard of York Gave Battle in Vain), or a version of this story:

December 1460: Richard of York has been named heir to King Henry VI – but the enraged Queen, Margaret of Anjou, has mustered a mighty army to oppose him and restore the succession to her son Edward, Prince of Wales. The hostile factions spend Christmas in Yorkshire, the Lancastrians at Pontefract Castle, and York at Sandal Castle; since food is short, many of his people go scouring the country for supplies. Meanwhile the Queen's forces take up position south of Wakefield and send heralds with insulting messages. Duke Richard is furious.

"They're too many to fight, Your Grace," says Sir Davy Halle, his old servant and counsellor, "Better wait till your son Edward brings reinforcements."

"Ah, Davy, Davy," says York, "Thou never saw me keep fortress when I was Regent of Normandy… should I, for dread of a scolding woman, incarcerate myself and shut my gates? My mind is rather to die with honour than live with shame! Their great number shall not appal my spirits but encourage them; for surely I have as many friends there as enemies, which at joining will either fly or take my part- hold hard, what's this?" (He peers from the battlements). "My foragers are being attacked - we must rescue them!"

With that the gallant Duke leads his army into the field. Alas for York, the enemy have hidden troops in nearby woodland; out they charge and surround his small force as if it were a fish in a net or a deer in a buck-stall!

"Flee, my son!" he cries to the 12-year-old Earl of Rutland, watching from the sidelines with his tutor, Robert Aspall. Edmund runs for Wakefield but is overtaken at the bridge by Lord Clifford. He kneels, imploring mercy.

"Spare him," cries Aspall, "He is a prince's son, and may do you good hereafter."

"Pah," replies Clifford, "By God's Blood, thy father slew mine at St Albans, and so I will do thee and all thy kin!" He strikes the helpless boy dead with his dagger, then captures the Duke and brings him to Queen Margaret.

"Madam, your war is done – here's your king's ransom!" say her nobles, perching Richard on an ant-hill, crowned with a paper crown.

"Now he looks like a king," she laughs contemptuously. "Off with his head - and plant it on Mickelgate Bar, so that York might overlook York!"[1]

Elements of this tale surface so frequently in accounts of the Battle of Wakefield that Richard of York has become a byword for failure: a man who through ignorance or stupidity led his son and followers on a mad charge from his castle only to be crushed by superior forces.[2] To some Victorian writers the Duke was a doomed romantic hero; today he is often considered rash, misguided or ill-prepared, while even broadly sympathetic accounts tend to denigrate him as a poor commander largely responsible for his own defeat.

But can this be true? Certainly Wakefield was a disaster for the Yorkists, costing them Duke Richard, the Earls of Rutland and Salisbury, numerous knights and squires and many others. Beyond that little is known, because traces of the battle are so scanty: a few 15th and 16th century reports of varying degrees of reliability, often ambiguous and inconsistent; a battlefield largely obliterated by Victorian and later development; and a handful of artefacts, some of doubtful provenance, mostly lost since their unearthing.[3] From this limited material, historians have extrapolated assumptions and in some cases, outright invention, in attempts to explain York's conduct at Wakefield. Mistakes have been accepted and embroidered, original sources misread or over-interpreted, theories accepted as facts, and received wisdom swallowed without sufficient consideration of its practical likelihood. The result is a substantial body of published work, disseminated increasingly via the Internet, which paints an unconvincing picture of the battle and cumulatively gives York a 'bad press'.[4]

This book seeks to redress the balance by unpicking various myths and presenting a different perspective on Richard of York: no fool or victim of his own misplaced heroism, but a prudent commander with a logical plan. It offers an alternative view of the battle based on the strongest evidence, allowing York's fatal decision to be seen more positively; and also attempts to treat other protagonists fairly by considering their personalities, context and possible motivations. Some might consider this futile; it has after all been said that, 'medieval men were not merely people of today clad in outlandish clothes and uttering dialect. Although they were biologically akin to us, their ways of thought were quite alien and their standards of political conduct were not ours. We cannot understand their civilisation by reading back our motives into past situations, but must instead try to grasp the ideas of their age.'[5] But our 15th century forebears were not a separate species to whom we are 'akin' - we are biologically *identical*, and share certain fundamentals of human nature: willingness to fight to the death for a cause; the striving of those with power to retain and extend it by any means; corruption and favouritism in ruling regimes; the influence of personality over politics; the failure to learn the lessons of history. These themes recur throughout the Wars of the Roses, and we can recognise and relate to them because they still persist today. So even at a distance of 550 years, if we regard those involved as beings like ourselves, subject to the same rational and irrational emotions, their psychology may be considered based on our elements of common experience. I believe that such a humanistic reappraisal enables us to better interpret the evidence and arrive at a more holistically credible version of history - their story.

Plate 2: A chivalric view of York's fall c. 1900; detail of polychrome plaster frieze by H.C. Fehr in the council chamber of Wakefield County Hall.

Notes

1. Culled from 16th century sources: Edward Halle, *The Union of the Two Noble Families of Lancaster and York*, folio xcix, 1550 edition, Scolar Press, 1970; Polydore Vergil, *Three Books of Polydore Vergil's English History*, Sir H. Ellis (ed.), Camden Society, 1844, pp. 108 - 9; William Shakespeare, *King Henry VI, Part 3.*

2. Indeed, the final chapter of P.A. Johnson's biography, *Duke Richard of York 1411 – 1460*, Oxford University Press, 1991, is entitled 'Failure'.

3. For the general reader, critical summaries and substantial extracts from primary sources can be found in Appendices II, VI and VII of *The Battle of Wakefield 1460*, Philip A. Haigh, Sutton Publishing Ltd., 1996; and *Henry VI, Margaret of Anjou and the Wars of the Roses: A Source Book*, Keith Dockray, Sutton Publishing Ltd., 2000.

4. For example, www.wars-of-the-roses.com : 'York decided to settle in [at Sandal Castle] for the winter and put his men to digging ditches, improving the defences and mounting guns on the walls. Thus entrenched in near-impregnable positions the Duke sat down to wait for reinforcements. Though he could not distinguish their exact whereabouts, York knew there were five or more Lancastrian armies in the vicinity and dared not face battle… It seems most likely that one of his many foraging parties came under attack and York sallied out to save them'; while according to www.information-britain.co.uk '…at Sandal Castle they made merry, depleting supplies to the extent that on December 30th a foraging party had to be despatched. This was promptly beaten back by the Lancastrians'.

5. Michael Hicks, *Richard III*, Collins & Brown, 1991, p.19.

CHAPTER 1: ENTER THE PROTAGONISTS

Wakefield marked a turning point in the bitter struggle for supremacy between the rival royal houses of Lancaster and York, called in the medieval period the 'Cousins War' and better known today as the Wars of the Roses. The Wars were a protracted cycle of violence, usurpation and counter-usurpation which fell into several distinct phases:

1450 – 1460:	War for control of Henry VI
1461:	War to depose Henry VI
1469 – 1471:	War to reinstate Henry VI
1485 - 1487:	War between the Houses of York and Tudor[1]

How did this conflict arise – and within its framework, what specifically caused the Battle of Wakefield? The Tudor commentator Polydore Vergil placed the blame firmly on Richard of York, who 'had conceived an outrageous lust of principality, and never ceased to devise with himself how and by what means he might compass it.' But the truth is more complex[2] and the roots of the problem can be traced to the 14th century, when a dangerous precedent was set: the disposal of an unsatisfactory monarch.

Historical Prelude

From 1308 to 1327, the reign of Edward II was beset by unrest. This was largely due to his malleable character and ill-advised dispensation of favour, whereby personal friends (or as some contend, lovers) like Piers Gaveston and Sir Hugh Despenser were elevated to high office regardless of their competence. His reliance on their self-interested counsel caused resentment among the established nobility who eventually rebelled, and with the connivance of Edward's queen and her lover, forced him to abdicate in favour of his 14-year-old son - a deposition soon followed by his horrible murder.[3]

Youth notwithstanding, Edward III was a more virile character than his father – and the inadvertent catalyst for much that came later. By pressing his claims to rule France, the new Plantagenet king launched what became the Hundred Years War - a spectre destined to fatefully haunt his 15th century descendants. Married in 1328 to Philippa of Hainault, King Edward sired 12 children of whom five sons and four daughters survived to maturity; and by founding the Order of the Garter, introducing the rank of 'duke' (from the French *duc*) into England and awarding it to his sons, he created new royal houses and the potential for sibling rivalry of epic proportions. His eldest sons Edward (known as the 'Black Prince' for his black armour) and Lionel were made the first Dukes of Cornwall and Clarence respectively. A trusted captain, Henry of Grosmont, became Duke of Lancaster - a title subsequently inherited by the King's third son, John of Gaunt, upon his marriage to Blanche, Grosmont's daughter and heir. Finally in 1377 his fourth son, Edmund of Langley, became the first Duke of York and his fifth, Thomas of Woodstock, Duke of Gloucester[4] – titles bestowed not by their father but by his successor Richard II, the Black Prince's son.

King Richard had the misfortune to inherit his throne aged only ten, bereft of both his energetic and capable father, who died in 1376 of illness caught while campaigning in Spain, and his illustrious grandfather, who had succumbed in 1377 after years of poor health. During Richard's minority England was governed by his royal uncles, the Dukes of Lancaster and Gloucester, and as it drew to a close he displayed a certain precocious promise in his response to the 1381 Peasant's Revolt against the Poll Tax. However, like Edward II he went on to rule from the heart not the head, bestowing excessive privileges on favourites like John de Vere, Earl of Oxford, elevated to Duke of Ireland, and William de la Pole, the son of a Hull merchant, created Earl of Suffolk. The results were predictable: the rebellion of disaffected nobles in 1387, (led by Richard's uncle of Gloucester), and eventual deposition by his own cousin Henry Bolingbrook, John of Gaunt's son and heir to the duchy of Lancaster[5] – thus in 1399, when Bolingbrook assumed the throne as Henry IV, the first usurping dynasty was born.

(Incidentally, John of Gaunt's extra-marital activities introduced a new element into this already volatile family mix: the powerful, ambitious Beaufort clan, illegitimate offspring of his mistress Katherine Swynford. The Beauforts would play important political roles under Henrys IV, V and VI, prominent among them being John, Marquess of Somerset; Henry, Cardinal Beaufort and Bishop of Winchester; Thomas, Duke of Exeter; and Joan, who by her marriage to Ralph Neville, first Earl of Westmorland, would one day become the mother-in-law of Richard of York).

Meanwhile Richard II either died naturally, committed suicide by starving himself to death, or was murdered by deliberate starvation during his imprisonment in Pontefract Castle in 1400. Although many people welcomed the change from his erratic and autocratic rule, it did not follow that his Lancastrian replacement would enjoy a trouble-free reign. In fact Henry IV faced repeated uprisings by such erstwhile supporters as the powerful Percy family of Northumberland, together with a major rebellion in Wales led by Owain Glyndwr. Luckily he had a dynamic 16-year-old son, Henry of Monmouth, who cut his military teeth in 1403 fighting the rebellious Percys then consolidated his reputation as Lieutenant of Wales, in which capacity he helped defeat Owain Glyndwr and end the Welsh insurrection.

As his health began failing around 1406, Henry IV came to rely increasingly on this talented prince and gave him a seat on the royal council –

doubtless to develop his state-craft with an eye to the succession. The popular young Henry's own affinity developed correspondingly, until he was presiding over what amounted to a rival court. This was tolerated while Henry IV was too ill to fully exercise his power; but in 1412, when Monmouth sanctioned an expedition to France against his father's wishes, the King rallied, 'discharged the prince from his council'[6] and deprived him of his offices. Their ensuing strained relations may have eased as the year wore on and it became clear that King Henry would not live to impede his son's ambitions for much longer; only in fact until March 1413, whereupon the crown passed unchallenged to his 25-year-old heir. Sources suggest that Henry of Monmouth (ironically, raised in the court of Richard II) had been a boisterous youth, much given to sport, martial pursuits and roistering in taverns; but that on his accession he sobered up, rewarded and dismissed his dissolute companions, and henceforth kept close only those who had warned him about his previous behaviour.[7]

The truth of this is debatable, but beyond dispute is that Henry V took his new role very seriously. Unlike some, he applied himself to being not merely a king, but a *good* one; a ruler who, as God's anointed, defended Church and faith, dispensed justice without fear or favour; maintained peace, law and order at home; and abroad, safeguarded the kingdom and furthered its interests by battle if necessary. With two royal examples (Richard II and Henry IV) to draw from, well-grounded by his military career, the political and executive experience gained on his father's council, and doubtless aided by his good looks and robust physique, Henry V was equipped to deliver in every respect. Devout and orthodox, one of his early acts was a suppression of the Lollard heresy. Meticulous and determined, he took an active involvement in state affairs: listening to Parliament, addressing grievances and improving the administration of justice, stability in England being both his duty and an absolute necessity for the furtherance of his foreign policy. Indeed, Henry re-opened the Hundred Years War within months of ascending the throne, with the objective of recovering territories like Normandy and Acquitaine lost since Edward III's reign. Despite some grumbles about the resulting taxation, the French campaigns were generally popular; to ordinary soldiers they afforded employment and booty, and to the nobles, chance to fulfil their knightly potential, win glory and be rewarded by a grateful sovereign. For Henry V, they had an additional benefit: uniting the energies of his factious nobility in a common cause, handily diverting them from internecine strife and plots against his person.

Success in France served only to enhance Henry's position. In 1415 he captured Harfleur, a vital port in north-west France, and soon afterwards won a spectacular victory over French heavy cavalry at Agincourt.[8] He followed this up by conquering Normandy in 1417, and in 1420 the Treaty of Troyes named him Regent of France and successor to King Charles VI. The triumph was cemented by his marriage to Charles' daughter, Catherine of Valois, and the Lancastrian dynasty seemed assured when their healthy son was born in 1421. However, Henry V's ambitions to rule both England and France went unfulfilled; he contracted dysentery on campaign in 1422, and predeceased his father-in-law by a matter of weeks. His abrupt and untimely demise meant that for the third time in a century the English throne passed to a minor, this one the youngest of all: the nine-month-old Henry of Windsor.

King Henry VI

The third Lancastrian king was thus uniquely disadvantaged from his moment of accession. We cannot know whether, had he lived, his father's popularity would have continued, or whether Henry V could have met the challenge of wearing both crowns - although his proven attributes suggest he would have stood a better chance than most of succeeding. Either way, the conqueror of France had become a legend in his own lifetime, respected alike by friend and foe.[9] Had he lived, his son would at least have been raised with a model of strong, scrupulous kingship before him. But by dying at the height of achievement and renown, Henry V left only an impossible ideal to live up to and an impossible inheritance to manage - for within two months the French throne had also passed to his infant son (although Henry's formal coronation did not take place until 1431), a development greatly compounding the problems besetting his cradle. These centred on the late king's will and its last-minute provisions for the regencies of England and France during a long, and by that stage, plainly inevitable minority. Henry V had intended his younger brother Humphrey, Duke of Gloucester, to be guardian and regent in England, while his elder brother John, Duke of Bedford and heir-apparent to Henry VI, ruled in France. But to Gloucester's profound and ongoing chagrin, his political rivals (including his jealous older brother) opposed the appointment; he was recognised by parliament only as 'protector' with limited powers, and instead of ruling, received only a seat on the council where his will could easily be thwarted by a majority of his peers.[10]

Discord between these royal uncles simmered throughout Henry's infancy - a peculiar infancy necessitating his physical presence as monarch on certain official occasions.[11] Gloucester was also at odds with his own uncle, Cardinal Henry Beaufort, leading to some undignified skirmishing for power and custody of the child-king; and in 1426, the five-year-old Henry was required to preside over the opening of a parliament to resolve their differences. While it is impossible to know how much he understood, or was affected by, these family contentions, they may lie at the root of Henry's apparent life-long distaste for disharmony and conflict, and resultant attempts to placate those around him. (Sadly this did not include Duke Humphrey, whose treatment was to become one of the sores that festered so painfully for Richard of York).

So while by 15th century standards Henry VI received a normal upbringing for a royal child, to modern eyes it looks like a psychological disaster in the making. To begin with, he may have inherited a genetic disposition to mental ill-health from Charles VI (who laboured under the misapprehension that he was made of glass). Next he suffered two close family bereavements (father and maternal grandfather) within his first year, presumably exposing him to an environment of shock, grief, anxiety and commensurately increased expectations: as the only Lancastrian heir, everyone must have devoutly hoped that he would grow up to be 'a chip off the old block'. So Henry's was the strange fate of being an absolute monarch, yet utterly dependent upon his family for the first 15 years (almost half) of his reign. He therefore grew up beholden to, and undoubtedly grateful to, several sets of powerful and competitive relations: his paternal uncles, the Dukes of Bedford and Gloucester; his surviving Beaufort great-uncle Henry; his Beaufort cousins John and Edmund, successive Dukes of Somerset; his half-brothers Edmund and Jasper, products of his mother's second marriage to Owen Tudor; and of course his cousin-by-marriage, Richard of York.

Despite the grumbling backdrop of family quarrels, Henry's minority was managed competently enough by his uncles and council while his upbringing proceeded along conventional lines. His early years were spent in the care of the Dowager Queen and a largely female entourage including a principal nurse, day nurse, chamber-woman and laundress[12]; then at six, he was removed from his mother's household and placed under the tutelage of Richard Beauchamp, Earl of Warwick, for his education proper to begin. (This may have been normal practice; it does not necessarily follow that the transition was easy or painless). Initial auguries were good; a month short of his eighth birthday in 1429, Henry coped better with the prolonged ritual of coronation than the last child-king, Richard II having famously fallen asleep during his. A year later, he also seems to have coped with aplomb at his grandiose French coronation in Paris, and the ceremonials on his formal return into London.[13] Such problems as England faced so early in his reign, notably reversals in France and a dire shortage of money, (due to the campaigns against Joan of Arc, and two hugely expensive coronations), can hardly be laid at his door.

Perhaps the earliest portent of trouble can be seen in the Paston Letters, which show that by 1432, Warwick's charge had 'grown in years, in stature of his person and also in conceit and knowledge of his high and royal authority and estate... [causing] him more and more to grudge with chastising, and to loathe it'. Moreover, since Henry had 'been stirred by some from his learning, and spoken to of diverse matters not behovefull', the Earl requested that henceforth he, or one of his deputies, be present during Henry's meetings with other parties[14] - a request granted with the exception of 'such persons as for nighness of blood, and their estate, owe of reason to be suffered to speak with the king' (possibly the very persons causing the problems). This revealing document suggests that Henry possessed the arrogance of a monarch who considered himself above correction, (hence Warwick's understandable fear that his tutelage would one day be held against him), and the innocence of a youth susceptible to undesirable influences. Both traits persisted into his later life, inevitable consequences of being treated as an absolute ruler since his babyhood, coupled with constant exposure to the political power-plays of ambitious, sophisticated courtiers.

By 1434 Henry was clearly impatient to play a fuller part in state affairs, a desire from which his concerned privy council had to tactfully dissuade him,[15] but by 1436, privy seal writs and documents bearing the royal sign manual attest to his active involvement in government; and shortly before his 16th birthday in 1437, Henry VI assumed the full powers of personal kingship.[16] With that, the same flaws that had bedevilled the reigns of Edward II and Richard II set in: favouritism and the ill-considered exercise of patronage. From 1437, Henry distributed lands, properties and honours hand-over-fist, (at least 192 grants were doled out from 1437 – 1450), in some cases seriously under-estimating the cost to the crown, or simultaneously making the same award to more than one person. Why did he do this? Perhaps after so many years as king in little more than name, he wished to demonstrate his authority with princely magnanimity, especially to those he liked, felt beholden to and/or believed had served him well. It may have been a simple desire to please those around him; the insecure attempt of a fatherless youth to buy affection and approval; or a deliberate ploy to build his power-base by securing affinity and support (if the latter, it failed due to his beneficiaries' failure to exercise 'good lordship'). Alternatively, his indiscriminate bestowal of favours could be construed as the product of a chronically unassertive nature and an inability to refuse anything that was asked of him.

Whatever his motivation, Henry VI was apparently unable or unwilling to grasp the consequences of his actions, namely the depletion of crown resources, creation of factions and dangerous abuses of privilege by those closest to him. He plainly did not share his father's political shrewdness and aptitude for the minutiae of government; maybe he viewed such details as beneath his notice, or lacked the maturity and intellectual capacity to understand (although he was clearly not stupid in other respects); and whilst it was not his fault that many of his subjects were venal, exploitative and self-interested, it was his responsibility to recognise and act against such tendencies. Unfortunately King Henry did not, arguably *could* not, exert the necessary control – a fact obvious to those milking him for all they could get. His over-liberality resulted in a massive and expensive proliferation of the royal entourage, draining of the exchequer, and flagrant breaches of the law by household men who could manipulate his trusting, generally merciful nature into pardoning their offences. Predictably, this caused widespread lawlessness, loss of public confidence in the administration of justice, and resentment and frustration among less-favoured nobles.[17]

Meanwhile in his second kingdom, rebellions against English rule continued, and although Henry might have privately wished his French subjects to accept him as their rightful king, he lacked both the taste and the finances for a decisive war to enforce their submission. He was repeatedly outmanoeuvred, politically and militarily, by his maternal uncle Charles VII (who notwithstanding being bypassed in the succession, was crowned in Rheims in 1429); and despite – or perhaps because of – his attempts to broker peace by marrying a French princess, throughout the 1440's English-held territories in France were gradually eroded. The cost of campaigning, the loss of revenues from Maine, Anjou and Normandy, the return of thousands of defeated, demoralised and often destitute combatants and displaced persons exacerbated problems at home.[18] By 1449, the Lancastrian government was in serious trouble; sea-borne trade, and with it the economy, had suffered badly and widespread rumblings of discontent were breaking out into active rebellions.

England's ruler was no help, being better fitted by nature and inclination to an ecclesiastical or academic career than the supreme power thrust upon him by accident of birth. Henry VI seems to have been a likeable individual, possessed of admirable qualities including simplicity, generosity, mildness, chastity and piety. Unfortunately, the negative aspects of these virtues – naïveté, unthinking prodigality, weakness, excessive (and expensive) preoccupation with the spiritual rather than the temporal realm - did not make for an effective king, a fact not lost on contemporary commentators.[19] What may have been an open-minded willingness to heed others' opinions made Henry a weather-vane of a monarch; lacking the courage of his convictions, he was perpetually vulnerable to being manipulated by whoever had his ear at the time. Furthermore, he apparently could not distinguish between good and bad counsel, and both Humphrey of Gloucester and Richard of York fell victim to his tendency to be swayed by malicious propaganda. Possibly this difficulty in telling disinterest from self-interest resulted from his rarefied, sheltered and highly artificial upbringing, wherein he had no choice but to trust his household and council; and unlike the Lancastrian princes who succeeded as adults, no opportunity to develop independence of thought or action free from the stultifying pressure of the crown. That Henry VI was weak-minded is suggested by his extreme openness to persuasion and vacillating, indecisive policies, and confirmed by two serious mental breakdowns from which, arguably, he never fully recovered. The first may have occurred in response to England's defeat in the Hundred Years War and expulsion from France – the loss of all his father's gains, which could only have come as a great personal and national humiliation. His reaction was to withdraw into a form of catatonic stupor; for more than a year he could not speak or do anything for himself, and it is a tribute to the quality of 15th century nursing that he survived this collapse - and a second shorter episode in 1456 - at all.

For fans of the counterfactual, or 'what if', school of history, it is interesting to speculate what might have happened if the sixth Henry had been more like the fifth. The Hundred Years War would almost certainly have ended more favourably for England; the Duke of York's allegiance would not have been lost; the Prince of Wales would in due course have succeeded, and Edward IV been of the House of Lancaster, not York; we would have had no Richard III, no Tudor dynasty or Elizabethan period... As it was, 'nature and nurture' combined to produce an unfit ruler whose plight merits compassion as much as it provokes exasperation, because it first set his foot on the road to the Battle of Wakefield.

Queen Margaret of Anjou

Margaret of Anjou, the niece of Charles VII, was born in 1429 or 1430. Her parents were King René of Anjou, brother to Queen Marie of France, and Isabella, the heiress of Charles, Duke of Lorraine. The younger of two daughters who survived to maturity, Margaret's *raison d'être* was one she shared with all 15th century noblewomen: to make an advantageous marriage. In this respect her prospects could have been hindered by her father's relative impoverishment; although rich in titles, (King of Sicily, Naples, Hungary and Jerusalem, Count of Provence and Duke of Bar and Lorraine by right of his wife), René possessed little hard cash or lands beyond Anjou. However, the fate of this virtually dowerless princess changed dramatically in the mid 1440's, when she became a valuable pawn on the chessboard of Anglo-French politics. Offering Margaret as a spouse for his nephew suited Charles VII excellently: she would be a tool to retrieve English holdings in Anjou and Maine, and a sympathetic agent in the highest position at the English court.[20] It also suited Henry's aims; he too sought peace and diplomatic advantage, and being half Valois himself, perhaps naturally looked to France to provide his queen.

The marriage treaty was accordingly concluded in May 1444. Presumably Margaret was delighted, and deeply grateful to her uncle and father for brokering the match. Despite her dowry of only 20,000 francs, she would be catapulted to the pinnacle of the feminine hierarchy in a far more splendid marriage than she might have expected to make. Moreover, images of Henry VI suggest that his appearance was personable enough; he was also a fluent French speaker, gentle, affable, devout and notably chaste – Margaret's lot would not be the commonplace humiliation of a string of royal mistresses and 'Fitzroys' – and above all he was King of England, which by medieval standards would have been ample compensation for any number of sins and shortcomings.

Henry was probably equally pleased with his 15-year-old bride, described by the contemporary French chronicler Thomas Basin as 'good-looking and well-developed'; while in 1458, the envoy Raffaelo de Negra told the Duchess of Milan that Margaret, then in her late twenties, was said to be 'a most handsome woman' – albeit with the politic qualification, 'somewhat dark and not so beautiful as your Serenity'.[21] And while most contemporary images are stylised and convey little of her true appearance (see Plate 4), Margaret's attractiveness is borne out by a picture attributed to King René, a great patron of the arts and no mean painter himself, in his Book of Hours. A medal struck by Pietro de Milan in 1463 also shows a softly-rounded face with large eyes, a straight nose, full lips and abundant wavy hair.[22]

Plate 3: A young Margaret of Anjou, as depicted by her father René in his Book of Hours.

Whatever the couple's early impressions of one another, their wedding went ahead as planned and Margaret was received into London with tremendous pomp in May 1445. The experience may have been awe-inspiring and mightily gratifying for a young woman wholly untried in such a state capacity, but we do not know whether she appreciated the uneasiness of her new position. A marriage with 'the enemy', especially one who brought England no great financial assets, aroused distaste in certain quarters, along with the suspicion that she would try to influence her husband to further French interests. From the outset she also laboured under heavy expectations – made clear by the welcoming pageants emphasising her role as the bringer of peace and plenty.[23]

Her royal career began conventionally as Margaret applied herself to doing exactly what was expected of a 15th century queen: exercising 'good ladyship' through patronage and favour. As the cynics predicted, she also did exactly what they expected of a Frenchwoman: within a very short time of their marriage she was lobbying Henry VI for the surrender of territories in her homeland. This is confirmed by the couple's letters to Charles VII in December 1445, in which (regarding Maine) Margaret undertakes to 'do for your pleasure the best that we can do, as we have always done', while Henry agrees to cede Maine and Le Mans partly as a favour to his 'dear and well-beloved companion the queen, who has requested us to do this many times'.[24]

Was this an early sign of Margaret's intention to be politically active by dominating her husband? She was after all the product of two generations of strong women: her paternal grandmother Yolande, sometime regent in Anjou, and her mother Isabella of Lorraine, who had campaigned staunchly on King René's behalf while he was a captive awaiting ransom. Or was it simply her desire to gratify the family to whom she owed her exalted position - and simultaneously Henry VI, whose cause she had espoused along with his person and who was pursuing a conciliatory line towards France? No doubt Margaret wished to foster peace and goodwill between her new husband and her blood-family; perhaps she believed - genuinely, if a trifle naïvely – that by adding her voice to the pressure on Henry, she was serving the best interests of both countries. Whatever her motivation, it is unlikely that her persuasions did much to influence events set in motion by the 1444 truce of Tours, and reinforced by the marriage itself. Nonetheless, contemporary and later commentators *did* blame her for the loss of territory; in the 1450's, an Englishman complained to Raffaelo de Negra that King Henry had taken Margaret 'without any dowry, and even restored some lands which he held to her father', while Thomas Gascoigne observed that with her, 'England received nothing of goods, but the loss of Maine and Anjou… to the queen's father'.[25]

Foreign affairs aside, her surviving letters show Queen Margaret to have been largely concerned with helping suppliants obtain their desires, whether for an office, a spouse, charity or some other favour[26] – all activities involving her mediation or intercession, and entirely proper to her position. However, her instructions on their behalf were often imperious, like this letter to Lord Ferrers of Groby, and may not always have been well-received:

Right trusty and well beloved, we greet you well. And forasmuch as we be informed that your bailiff of Stebbing wrongfully vexeth, troubleth and oppresseth our tenants of our lordship of Stebbing, as well in usurping and breaking our franchise there as in other grievous wise; We do therefore desire and pray you, and also exhort and require you, that you do give in commandment to your said bailiff for to cease of his vexations and oppressing, and put him in such rule that our said tenants may live in rest and peace, so that they have no cause to complain again unto us for lack of remedy in your default, as you think to stand in the favour of our good grace, and to eschew our displeasure at your peril.[27]

She could also deliver a stinging rebuke to those who failed to obey, like the unfortunate Yeoman of the Crown, William Chaterley:

> *We marvel greatly that you durst presume… against our writing unto you in that matter, for to come into our park of Aggersley, there destroying our game, where we were disposed to have cherished you in your disport in our other places; wherefore we expressly charge you that from henceforward you come into none of our places and parks, neither to hunt nor serve warrant, without your especial commandment in that behalf, at your peril. For thus it pleases us to be done.*[28]

Another important example of Margaret's intercessions is her pleading for pardons for the Cade rebels[29] in 1450. Was this compassion or political expediency performed with gritted teeth? More likely the latter, since she had reason enough to be outraged: Cade's followers had challenged her husband's authority, insulted his cherished advisors and sought to replace them with the Duke of York. Nonetheless, it was prudent to put a gloss of queenly benevolence over pardons granted more to restore stability than for mercy's sake. It was all good for her public image, like her founding of Queen's College, Cambridge, in 1448 – one of the positive acts by which she is remembered today.

While Queen Margaret got to grips, for better or worse, with the diplomatic and administrative aspects of her position, in another vital respect she was failing national expectations by not delivering the required heir. There are several possible explanations for this. She was only 15 at the time of her marriage, and her menstrual cycle may not have been fully established; consummation may have been delayed for this reason, or to spare her the risk of youthful pregnancy. Or their sexual encounters may have been infrequent; the devout Henry would unquestionably have recognised his duty to procreate, but may have recoiled from indulging in carnality – perhaps to the extent of abstaining from intercourse on all the holy days proscribed by the Church, commensurately reducing their chances of conception. An indictment of 1447 hints at some such abstemious counsel: in it, a London draper alleges that the Bishop of Aiscough kept the King from 'having his sport' with the Queen[30] - although precisely *how* the Bishop, along with the Marquis of Suffolk and other lords accused, managed to distract or dissuade Henry from conjugal activities remains a matter for speculation. Alternatively, the inexperienced couple may have just been unlucky with their timing; or maybe other conceptions occurred, but went unreported because they miscarried so early that not even the Queen realised she had been pregnant.

This delay in fulfilling her ultimate wifely function gave rise to legitimate concerns regarding the succession and future security of the realm - and did little to enhance Margaret's popularity, for when she at last became pregnant after eight years of marriage, aspersions were cast on her son's paternity.[31] Could there be any truth in the gossip and Yorkist propaganda – was Margaret so desperate to consolidate her position that she turned to a more potent lover to father her child? Did the suspicion – or knowledge - that someone else was responsible for his wife's pregnancy contribute to the King's breakdown that same year? (On recovery Henry acknowledged the child as his own, which is hardly surprising; he loved and trusted Margaret, and was presumably delighted that they had done their duty by securing the succession. In the unlikely event that he suspected her of infidelity, he may not have considered it expedient to announce the fact with a major public scandal).

Plate 4: Queen Margaret at prayer, from a manuscript owned by The Skinners' Company and held in the Reference Library of the Guildhall, City of London. Photo by Ted Hall; reproduced by kind permission of The Skinners' Company.

In the absence of conclusive DNA proof we cannot be absolutely certain, although it is perfectly possible, arguably most likely, that Prince Edward was legitimate. His birth on 13th October suggests that he was conceived around mid-

January 1453 – a time his parents are known to have been together at Greenwich for the knightly investiture of the King's Tudor half-brothers. Moreover, Henry's breakdown did not take place until July or August, when he would have known of Margaret's condition for several months; if the advancing pregnancy *did* contribute to his collapse, a more feasible reason is anxiety about his wife and child's survival, rather than shock over the belated realisation that he had been cuckolded.

The delivery of a healthy son fundamentally altered the political landscape of the 1450's and heralded a new phase of political life for Queen Margaret. Hitherto, Humphrey of Gloucester had been heir-presumptive to the King, then several years after his death in 1447, Richard of York was acknowledged as heir-apparent; now, with Prince Edward's birth, the Duke was effectively demoted. Given the deterioration in their relationship since the events of 1450, we can easily imagine the Queen's glee at displacing York with her own child – albeit tempered by the consternation she surely felt over Henry's illness, which for nine months rendered him incapable of recognising his son.

In modern terms, Queen Margaret's response to the situation seems natural and understandable: she wished to act as regent during her husband's incapacity, female regency being a precedent set by her grandmother Yolande. Sadly for Margaret, in 15th century England this was an unthinkable threat to the entrenched, biblically-ordained structure of patriarchal power, and in 1454 her desire was thwarted in the most galling way imaginable: after a good deal of parliamentary wrangling, the in-law who had become her arch-rival, Richard of York, was acknowledged Protector of England.

Richard, Duke of York

Born in 1411, Richard of York was orphaned at an early age. His mother Anne Mortimer was a descendant of Edward III, (the great-granddaughter of Lionel, first Duke of Clarence), and died shortly after his birth; his father Richard was executed in 1415, possibly the victim of a rare miscalculation on behalf of Henry V. York's father was also descended from Edward III, being the second son of Edmund of Langley, Duke of York. In 1414 his position as heir to his childless brother Edward, second Duke of York, was recognised when Henry V created him Earl of Cambridge – with the expectation that Richard would merit the elevation through service on Henry's French campaigns. The new Earl was thereby placed in an awkward position, since his title had brought with it no lands or money, and he could not afford to equip himself for military service in the style commensurate with his rank. His resulting dissatisfaction and resentment may well have led to an ill-advised conspiracy with other disgruntled nobles in the so-called 'Southampton Plot', a wholly impractical plan to depose Henry V in favour of Richard's brother-in-law Edmund Mortimer, Earl of March. However, recognising the plot's futility,

March saved his own life by betraying it; Cambridge was duly attainted and executed along with his co-conspirators in August 1415.[32] Possibly King Henry felt a twinge of conscience over the treatment that had alienated Cambridge and prompted his disastrous rebellion; the late Earl's attainder was not perpetuated in his son, who was raised as a ward of the crown and shortly inherited the dukedom of York when Edward of Langley died at Agincourt (although many of the lands and estates were granted to others to manage and benefit from during his minority).

Little is known of Richard of York's childhood. Plainly, he could not have known his mother, and we can only speculate on his feelings about the father who died when he was four, and whose conduct was roundly condemned by contemporaries;[33] that Richard did not blame Henry V for his father's death, indeed may have been brought up hero-worshipping the warrior king, is suggested by his later vigorous defence of Henry's French conquests. We do know that his earliest years were spent in the custody of Robert Waterton, Constable of Pontefract Castle, as evinced by a petition in 1422 for £100 for the Duke's allowance, and a further assignment allocated in 1423. Later that year, Richard's tutelage passed to the indefatigable dynast Ralph Neville, Earl of Westmorland, who effectively 'bought' the 12-year-old from the crown for 3,000 marks as a husband for his youngest daughter, Cecily.[34]

Plate 5: Detail of painted glass from the 'Neville Window' at St Andrew's Church, Penrith. Assembled in the late 19th century, the window features two medieval portraits identified as Richard of York and Cecily Neville. However, they are more likely to represent York's parents-in-law, Ralph, Earl of Westmorland and Joan Beaufort. [35] Photo by Alistair Harper.

Acquiring the adolescent Duke as a son-in-law proved to be an excellent investment for the Nevilles, since in 1425 York was further enriched by inheriting the vast Mortimer estates of his childless maternal uncle – somewhat ironically, that same Earl of March with whom his father had so unwisely sought to replace Henry V.

Thus Richard did not start out as the figurehead of a Yorkist faction or a rival for the throne but as the King's loyal servant, a Lancastrian ward married into a prominent Lancastrian family. His mother-in-law Joan Beaufort was John of Gaunt's daughter, and therefore King Henry's great-aunt, and his early career proceeded as expected for one allied to the throne both by kinship and marriage. In 1426, York was one of 23 noblemen knighted by and with their five-year-old sovereign at Leicester, and in April 1428 he was removed from the widowed Countess of Westmorland's household to reside continuously at court. Richard was presumably involved with the ceremonials surrounding Henry VI's coronation in 1429, as a grant of 200 marks made from his Welsh estates at this time seems to indicate; and he received a further 500 marks in 1430, to finance the provision of 12 lances and 36 archers to add to the retinue for Henry's French coronation. That same year he also enjoyed his first high-level appointment, an apparently short-lived stint as Constable of England to preside over a duel between John Upton and John Donne.[36]

On returning from France in 1432, the 21-year-old Richard's first priority was petitioning for livery and authority of estates inherited from the late Duke of York and Earl of March, including lands in Ireland, Yorkshire, the Midlands, East Anglia and the Welsh marches.[37]Assuming control of these widely-dispersed holdings must have occupied a good deal of his time and energy in the 1430's; meanwhile his ceremonial and political role developed with his creation as a Knight of the Garter in 1433, and his interim appointment as Lieutenant and Governor General of France in 1436 (to replace King Henry's uncle Bedford, since whose death in 1435 England had lost Dieppe and suffered a serious uprising in the Pays de Caux region of Normandy). York performed competently in this, his first major commission, recovering Fécamp and re-establishing control in the Pays de Caux; he was appointed Captain of Rouen in January 1437, and the following month recaptured Pontoise, a key town on the Seine, before being succeeded in the office by the Earl of Warwick.[38]

Back in England, York was agreeably occupied on the domestic front: in 1438, Duchess Cecily conceived after 14 years of marriage and perhaps eight of actively trying (she was only nine at the time of their wedding, so the consummation would have been considerably delayed). 1439 must therefore have been a happy year for the couple, as February saw Richard's appointment to the royal council and May, doubtless to their mutual joy and relief, the arrival of a healthy firstborn:

> *Aftir the tyme of longe bareynesse,*
> *God first sent Anne, which signyfieth grace,*
> *In token that al her hertis hevynesse*
> *He, as for bareynesse, wold fro hem chace* [39]

Indeed, the years 1438 - 1439 may have been one of the happiest interludes in Richard's life. Now in his late twenties, he was a premier magnate and one of the richest men in England. He had just proved himself as a soldier and administrator on behalf of his sovereign in Normandy; proved his beautiful wife (Cecily's nickname was 'the Rose of Raby') fertile at last; and furthermore managed to avoid becoming overly embroiled in the acrimonious disputes between Humphrey of Gloucester and Cardinal Beaufort. But his contentment was not to last. The Earl of Warwick died in April 1439 so a new Lieutenant of France had to be found; and since Gloucester's appointment was opposed by the Beauforts, York, either by virtue of his experience and credentials or simply by default, was the only realistic candidate for the office.

Initially, all seemed well. He was formally reappointed on a five-year term in July 1440, by which time he may have known, or at least suspected, that his Duchess was pregnant again; and his amicable relations with King and council are suggested by a reward for good service in November 1440, whereby five of his towns in Hertfordshire, Kent and Buckinghamshire were relieved of the duty of victualling any man or officer for ten years.[40] Meanwhile the Duke appointed a council to represent him in England,[41] a judicious mix of prominent lay and ecclesiastical figures close to Henry VI, (like the King's then confessor, the Bishop of Salisbury), but not identified too strongly either with the Duke of Gloucester or Cardinal Beaufort; and attempted to pin down the terms of his office, which were essentially to hold Normandy, with English support, until a peace could be arranged. An advance party of 200 men-at-arms and archers was duly dispatched in September 1440, with York himself expected to follow in April 1441. In the event, his arrival was delayed until June due to problems in raising the muster and obtaining adequate ordnance, together with a personal crisis: in February 1441 his first son, Henry, (presumably named in honour of the King), died shortly after birth.

When the Duke finally arrived in Normandy, he established his base at Rouen and installed his Duchess. (By the standards of the time, the Yorks seem to have enjoyed a close, maybe deeply loving relationship; they had after all been companions for nigh on 20 years, and Cecily frequently accompanied Richard on his postings. They also plainly enjoyed a regular sex-life; notwithstanding the loss of their baby, the Duchess soon conceived again and bore another son, Edward, in April 1442 – the first of two healthy sons and a daughter who would arrive during their French sojourn). Richard then embarked on a campaign to relieve Pontoise, experiencing some short-term successes although a lack of resources, both on land

and at sea, rendered it impossible to press the advantage or re-take the key port of Dieppe despite a prolonged siege. His policy was perforce largely defensive, and he also attempted to restore good order by touring the regions and addressing local grievances.

Back in England, there were complaints about cost (York was paid the then colossal sum of £20,000 for 1441 – 1442, though he was still owed over 1,000 marks for expenses from his first lieutenancy and got no further payment till 1444), lack of tangible results, and the harassment of English shipping by French and Breton sailors.[42] During 1442, the situation worsened as Charles VII and his son set out to re-conquer English Gascony, leading to heated debate in King Henry's council regarding which duchy to relieve: Normandy, Gascony, or both. In the end, 'from this background of competing claims... emerged the ultimate English plan, not of aid to existing hard-pressed areas but of new aggression and conquest in areas between Gascony and Normandy'.[43] This appears to have been a self-interested policy driven by the new Duke of Somerset, John Beaufort, (appointed commander-in-chief), with the object of carving himself a patrimony in Anjou, Maine and Alençon – although his expedition was presented as a mobile shield and defence for the threatened duchies, and a development which intended York no 'disworship'.[44] Resources ear-marked for Richard's defence of Normandy were diverted to this fresh cause and after long and costly delays, Somerset eventually arrived at Cherbourg in August 1443 with a force of around 8,000 men. His first action was to sack La Guerche, prompting aggrieved complaint from the Duke of Brittany and jeopardising the vital but fragile Anglo-Breton alliance, before moving on to ravage lands between Normandy and the Loire. In the process he lost troops and equipment and failed to engage any major French field forces; arguably his activities prevented Charles VII from pressing the attack on Gascony, but this represented little return on such an expensive venture and Somerset returned ignominiously to England, where he died in May 1444.

The whole fiasco must have been profoundly galling to York. Despite reassurances to the contrary, there was implicit criticism in the appointment of a second senior commander in France. The sanctioning of Somerset's abortive attempt to wage 'cruel and mortal war' made a mockery of his own struggles to regain control in Normandy, and squandered valuable resources he could have deployed to far better effect. Moreover, the blithe granting of all Somerset's demanding pre-conditions of service - which his subsequent performance had failed to justify – contrasted sharply with the way York felt he was being treated, and may have contributed to his catastrophic resentment against Henry's Beaufort relations.

Meanwhile attempts to reach a negotiated settlement creaked on, buying a two-year truce with Henry's marriage to Margaret of Anjou – and incidentally bringing York face-to-face with his future adversary for the first time. What they made of each other on a personal level is anyone's guess; the Duke and Duchess of

York, respectively aged 34 and 30, were old enough to be the teenager's parents, and presumably Margaret accepted them at face value as senior members of her new husband's nobility. But whatever their feelings, duty and ceremonial were carried out: York met the princess at Pontoise in March 1445, entertained her entourage at Rouen over Easter, escorted her to Honfleur for her bridal journey[45] – and in 1446, named his next daughter Margaret, possibly in her honour.

On returning to England in 1445, York left Normandy defensible and governable, but soon found himself faced with allegations of mismanagement by Adam Moleyns, Bishop of Chichester and Keeper of the Privy Seal. The Duke had to petition King Henry to be allowed to answer these criticisms in parliament, and rebut accusations of favouritism in the payment of wages by stating that he had paid what he could with the resources available - York himself being owed thousands of pounds by the exchequer.[46] It must have been a disquieting situation, revealing that he had detractors if not outright enemies among those close to the King. Nonetheless, in September 1446 he was appointed Steward and Chief Justice of the royal forests south of the Trent, and in December, as a reward for good service, received a licence to hold weekly markets and an annual fair at his town of Bewdley in Gloucestershire.[47] However, most likely to his great disappointment and contrary to his expectations, York was not re-appointed as Lieutenant of France. Instead the office went to the new Duke of Somerset, Edmund Beaufort, younger brother of the John whose 1443 expedition had proved such a costly failure.

An even more disquieting situation arose in January 1447 when Humphrey of Gloucester, whose hawkish policies towards France had put him at odds with the King and Cardinal Beaufort, was arrested and died under suspicious circumstances. Gloucester had been increasingly out of favour for some years, tainted by association with his wife Eleanor Cobham's ill-advised occult dabbling and attempts to predict Henry's death (for which she was stringently punished and divorced from the Duke in 1441); in 1460, York was to claim not only that Gloucester was murdered, but that those responsible also proposed to murder him.[48] Whether or not his suspicions were justified, it does appear that by the mid-1440's, there were moves by the court faction to discredit and marginalise him; in July 1447 he was created Lieutenant of Ireland, a logical enough appointment in terms of his holdings there, but viewed by some contemporaries as tantamount to exile because he had opposed King Henry's surrender of Maine and financial settlements made on the Beauforts.[49] Either way, Richard did not rush to accept the appointment, although he had reasons other than simple rancour for delaying his departure until July 1449: the necessity to put down serious disorder on his Welsh lands during 1448, and the deaths of two infant sons (William in late summer 1447 and John in November 1448) to contend with.

On arriving in Ireland as Earl of Ulster in his own right, Richard promptly set about establishing his military authority, suppressing rebellions and obtaining the submission of Irish chieftains to Henry VI's rule. His lieutenancy was largely successful in imposing good governance, and his removal from the political mainstream absolved him from responsibility for the progressive losses in France. Unfortunately it did nothing to ameliorate the dismissive treatment he was receiving, (for instance the exchequer neglected to pay his salary, causing him financial embarrassment). Nor did it halt the whispering campaign against him, and from 1450 onwards his relationship with the English court took a sharp turn for the worse.

In summary, early relations between the Duke, King and Queen were amicable enough – although Henry VI and his household may always have felt uneasy about York's lineage and potential claim to the throne, especially once he started to produce sons while the King remained childless. So it would have behoved the House of Lancaster to keep this mighty subject 'on side', especially as York had done his duty, serving Henry to the best of his ability; nonetheless, if not simple bureaucratic incompetence, the first intimations of dislike or discrimination are suggested by the non payment of his expenses in 1442 – 43. Whether the Duke performed well or badly in Normandy remains, as it was at the time, a matter of opinion,[50] but added to any pre-existing clash of personalities, a root cause of the growing estrangement between King Henry's Yorkist and Lancastrian relations surely lies in their bitter disputes about the conduct of military affairs in France. Matters of war are notoriously easy to argue about, and both sides no doubt felt equally justified in accusing the other of mismanagement, their disagreements over policy issues spilling out into personal enmity and fuelling a downward spiral of misunderstanding, suspicion and hatred.

Exposed to constant grumbles about the Duke's lack of progress, King Henry apparently came to share his household's view - because York's reward for his service, and for bankrolling the garrison from his own pocket, was not the gratitude and affection he might reasonably have expected. Instead he received tardy and grudging repayment; the lack of confidence and tacit rebuke implied by John Beaufort's appointment as a second commander-in-chief; failure to renew his lieutenancy; exclusion from Henry's inner circle; and finally the effective banishment of being packed off to Ireland.

Why did this happen? Henry VI could be admirably loyal to those who served him - but it was a selective loyalty, as evinced by his treatment of Humphrey of Gloucester. Perhaps his favour was influenced by proximity and familiarity; perhaps he found the Beauforts, excluded from the succession as a bastard line, less threatening to his position; perhaps they were more polished sycophants than York, who may have been somewhat haughty in his pride of lineage and plainly did not suffer fools gladly; perhaps he simply liked them better.

Certainly things were not well by 1445, when criticism of York by the court faction, and *vice versa*, had become overt. Richard may have been unfair in blaming English losses in France on the successive Dukes of Somerset - arguably the endeavour was doomed from the start, the cost and logistical problems of retaining the second kingdom being so huge, and the wish of its populace to be ruled by a French king being ever-present - but it would have been treasonable to place the blame for England's weak foreign policy where it truly lay, with King Henry. Such criticism of God's anointed could be fatal; however, by the 1450's matters had become so desperate that many people – among them Richard of York – were prepared to risk clamouring for reform.

Notes

1. For alternative views on the phases of the Wars of the Roses, see for example John Gillingham, *The Wars of the Roses: Peace & Conflict in 15th Century England*, Phoenix Press, 2002, pp. xiv – xv.
2. Vergil, *op cit*, p.94; whether he truly believed this, or (writing in the reigns of Henrys VII and VIII), was taking the expedient Tudor party line, is open to question. Either way, the origin and cause of the wars, and the precise points at which they started and ended, has been a matter of debate since the 15th century – Dockray, *op cit*, 2000, pp. 27 – 40, gives an excellent summary of the various viewpoints.
3. J.R.S. Phillips, 'Edward II (1284 – 1327), *Oxford Dictionary of National Biography*, Oxford University Press, online edition, January 2008.
4. W.M. Ormrod, 'Edward III (1312 – 1377)', *Oxford Dictionary of National Biography*, Oxford University Press, online edition, January 2008.
5. Anthony Tuck, 'Richard II (1367 – 1400)', *Oxford Dictionary of National Biography*, Oxford University Press, online edition, January 2009.
6. According to the chronicler John Harding, quoted by Keith Dockray in *Warrior King: The Life of Henry V*, Tempus Publishing, 2007, p. 89.
7. *Ibid*, pp. 96 – 7.
8. Vividly described by Robert Hardy in *Longbow: A social and military history*, Patrick Stephens Ltd., 1996, pp. 96 – 120.
9. See Dockray, *op cit*, 2007, for contemporary English and French perspectives on Henry V.
10. Bertram Wolffe, *Henry VI*, Eyre Methuen, 1981, pp. 29 – 47.
11. *Ibid*, pp. 33 – 34.
12. *Ibid*, p. 36.
13. *Ibid*, pp. 60 – 64.
14. *Articles de Monsr. De Warrewyk touchant le bon regime du Roy,* 9th November 1432, in the *Paston Letters*, Vol. 1, J. Gairdner (ed.), Archibald Constable & Co., 1900, pp.31 – 35.
15. Wolffe, *op cit*, p. 80.

16. *Ibid*, p. 87.
17. *Ibid* - a full account of Henry VI's proliferating household, indiscriminate favours and ineffective exercise of judicial power can be found in Chapters 6 and 7.
18. *Ibid*, p. 211.
19. *Ibid*, pp. 3 – 21, and Dockray, *op cit*, 2000, pp. 1 – 10, quote contrasting views of Henry VI from contemporary and later sources. According to one chronicler, Henry was 'simple and led by covetous counsel, and owed more than he was worth'; *An English Chronicle of the Reigns of Richard II, Henry IV, Henry V and Henry VI*, ed. J.S. Davies, Camden Society, 1856, p. 79.
20. Wolffe, *op cit*, pp. 171 – 174.
21. Quoted in Dockray, *op cit*, 2000, p. xxviii and p. 15.
22. Reproductions of the medal can be found in A.W. Boardman, *The Battle of Towton*, Alan Sutton Publishing Ltd., 1994, p. 24, and of both portrait and medal in Wolffe, *op cit*, Plates 13 (b) and 13 (c).
23. Helen E. Maurer, *Margaret of Anjou: Queenship and Power in Late Medieval England*, Boydell & Brewer, 2003, pp. 19 – 23.
24. *Ibid*, pp. 31 – 33.
25. *Calendar of the State Papers of Milan*, and Gascoigne's *Loci et Libro*, quoted in *ibid,* p. 27.
26. *Ibid*, pp. 54 – 57.
27. *Letters of Queen Margaret of Anjou and Bishop Beckingham and Others, Written in the Reigns of Henry V and Henry VI*, Cecil Monro (ed.), Camden Society, 1968, pp. 146 – 147.
28. *Ibid*, p. 143.
29. Wolffe, *op cit*, p. 237 – 238.
30. *Ibid*, p. 17.
31. See Maurer, *op cit*, pp. 42 – 43.
32. G. L. Harriss, 'Richard, Earl of Cambridge, 1385 – 1415', *Oxford Dictionary of National Biography*, Oxford University Press, on-line edition, 2008.
33. Dockray, *op cit*, 2007, pp. 111 – 115.
34. Calendar of Patent Rolls, cited by Ian Postlethwaite in *Richard, Third Duke of York*, Yorkshire Branch of the Richard III Society, 1974, p.2.
35. Ralph Neville, the fourth Lord of Raby, was created Earl of Westmorland by Richard II in 1397, and granted the Honour of Penrith. He probably rebuilt the collapsed church at Penrith, and created a window incorporating portraits of himself, his wife and the arms of Neville. These elements were retained when St Andrew's was rebuilt in 1720, and later placed in a new south window where they are misidentified as the Duke and Duchess of York. I am indebted to Mr. Jeremy Godwin of Penrith for this information.

36. Postlethwaite, *op cit*, p. 4.
37. For a detailed discussion of York's inheritance, income and estate administration, see Johnson, *op cit*, pp. 1 – 27.
38. Postlethwaite, *op cit*, p.8.
39. The opening of a contemporary verse listing all the Yorks' children, quoted in P.W. Hammond & Anne F. Sutton, *Richard III: The road to Bosworth Field*, Guild Publishing, London, 1985, p.23.
40. Postlethwaite, *op cit*, p.9.
41. Johnson, *op cit*, p.34.
42. Wolffe, *op cit*, p. 154.
43. *Ibid*, p. 162.
44. *Ibid*, p. 166.
45. Johnson, *op cit*, pp. 46 – 47.
46. *Ibid*, pp. 51 – 62.
47. Postlethwaite, *op cit*, p. 14.
48. Johnson, *op cit*, p. 66. For a full account of the Gloucesters' spectacular fall from grace, see Ralph A. Griffiths, 'The Trial of Eleanor Cobham: an Episode in the Fall of Duke Humphrey of Gloucester' in *King and Country: England and Wales in the Fifteenth Century*, Hambledon Press, 1991, pp. 233 – 252.
49. *Ibid*, p. 70. William Gregory, Mayor of London in 1451, was of this opinion: 'the said Duke was before banished for certain years with a notable fellowship' in the 'Chronicle of William Gregory, Skinner', *Historical Collections of a Citizen of London in the Fifteenth Century*, J. Gairdner (ed.), Camden Society, 1876, p. 195.
50. Dockray, *op cit*, 2000, gives a penetrating summary of views past and present on the Duke of York.

CHAPTER 2: THE ROAD TO WAR

The Turbulent 1450's

Harbinger of a turbulent decade, 1450 was a true *annus horribilis* for Henry VI. January saw the murder of his Keeper of the Privy Seal, Adam Moleyns, by resentful, unpaid soldiers in Portsmouth – among them one Cuthbert Colville, an esquire formerly in the Duke of York's service in Normandy.[1] The dying Moleyns apparently accused Henry's chief advisor William de la Pole, Duke of Suffolk, of responsibility for the surrender of Maine (as disgruntled English troops believed) and treachery with the French. This precipitated a parliamentary revolt against agents of the King's rule, and Suffolk was impeached for high treason on February 7th for conspiring with Charles VII and 'ymagynyng and purposing falsly and treytorously to destroy your moste roiall persone, and this your seid realme.'[2] Subsequent allegations included large scale financial mismanagement and profiteering, in which respect Suffolk was made the scapegoat for the corruption of royal officers and indirectly, the King's own failings.[3]

Much as he might have wanted to, Henry could not ignore it and committed Suffolk to the Tower of London, at least partly for his own protection. Declining to have him tried and condemned, the King instead banished him for five years; however, as the Paston letters relate, sailors from the ship *Nicholas of the Tower* exacted rough justice by beheading the hapless Duke at Dover on his way into exile.[4]

Attacks on the Lancastrian regime were thus becoming widespread, overt and violent. Political songs lampooned the excesses of his officers and even criticised Henry himself:

O rex, si rex es, rege te, vel eris sine re rex:
Nomen habes sine re, nisi te recte regas [5]

('O king, if king you be, rule yourself or you will be king without substance; you have the name without the reality unless you rule yourself rightly').

Meanwhile, notwithstanding his removal to Ireland, the Duke of York's presence was being felt alarmingly. With or without his knowledge and contrivance, malcontents desirous of political reform – or a new monarch – were bandying his name about; and in April, a sailor named Harries threshed before King Henry with a flail to show how York would 'fight with traytours at Leicester parliament and so thrashe them downe as he had thrashed the clods of erthe', a demonstration that earned him a traitor's death.[6] Next month York's name was invoked again by John ('Jack') Cade who, variously calling himself 'John Amend-all' or 'John Mortimer' and claiming to be the Duke's cousin, led a serious uprising from Kent and East Sussex to petition the King. 'Cade's Rebellion' involved several thousand respectable but deeply aggrieved citizens including esquires, gentlemen, yeomen, constables, tradesmen and artisans who collectively requested Henry to:

- Resume his lost French demesnes to re-establish his power and dignity (and, incidentally, to protect their interests by safeguarding the south-east and Channel against piracy and the threat of invasion from Normandy)
- Banish Suffolk's affinity and replace them by other lords of his blood, specifically to take about him 'a nobill persone, the trewe blode of the Reame, that is to say the hye and mighty prince the Duke of York, late exiled from our soueraigne lordes presens of the false traitour Duke of Southfolke and his affinite'[7]
- Punish those responsible for Humphrey of Gloucester's death and the loss of English possessions in France
- Prevent abuses of the law and corruption by household men

The King initially refused to consider these demands, and mustering a sizeable force of his own, rode out to confront the rebels at Blackheath. Cade's assembly, unwilling to face their sovereign in battle, dispersed overnight, whereupon Henry instructed his vanguard to hunt them down in the Kentish countryside. This foray cost him many men including two of the Duke of Buckingham's kinsmen; and next day, when he bade his army continue the pursuit they mutinied, taking up the rebel cry of 'destroy the traitors about the king.'[8] Faced with this insurrection Henry backed down, acted upon the petition and pardoned many of the insurgents. In the meantime came attacks on the Abbots of Gloucester and Hyde and the Bishops of Coventry, Norwich and Bath and Wells, while William Aiscough, Bishop of Salisbury, and Robert Russell, councillor of the late Adam Moleyns, were both killed; and in August, one William Brenchenham asserted that the Duke of York intended to return from Ireland and claim the throne.[9]

So Richard was far from alone in his distaste for Beaufort-influenced policies, but any gratification he felt at such manifestations of popular support was surely tempered by dismay at their treasonable implications. Although he may have privately harboured the conviction that he could do a better job than Henry VI – he could hardly do worse – York was not, at that stage, prepared to pursue his own claim to rule. Instead, in such urgent anxiety that he did not seek royal permission, (perhaps fearing it would be refused), he set forth for England to clear his name. These actions, which seemed to confirm abounding rumour, understandably caused great consternation among the King's affinity - no doubt compounded by fear that in such a climate, any forcible attempt on the throne might succeed. Henry's officers in Wales accordingly tried to impede the Duke's landing at Beaumaris and (York alleged) to imprison or execute some of his retinue, including himself. Richard promptly dispatched an open communication to the King, stating that:

...I have bin informed that diverse language hath bene said of me to your moste excellente estate whiche shoulde sounde to my dishonour and reproach... I have bene, and ever will be, your true liegeman and servaunte: and if there be any man that wyll or dare say the contrarie, or charge me otherwise, I beseech your rightwisenesse to call him before your high presence, and I wyll declare me for my discharge as a true Knighte ought to do...

He continued with complaints about the opposition to his landing, and concluded:

...above alle these wronges and iniures above said and doon unto me of malice withouten any cause, I being in your land of Ireland in your service... certtcyn personus laboured instantly forto have endited me of treson, to thentent to have undo me, myn issue and corrupt my blode, as it is opynly publisched. Besekyng your maieste rial of your rightwisnesse to do examyn thees maters and thereupon to do such justice in this behalve as the cause requireth...[10]

By late September York had reached London to plead his case directly to the King, who admitted him as 'oure trewe faithful subiecte and as our weel bilovid cosyn.'[11] So far, so good: the Duke had aired his concerns and Henry VI had, on the face of it, listened and accepted his protestations of loyalty. Perhaps this, coupled with his physical proximity to court, (he had taken up lodgings in the Bishop of Salisbury's house), made Richard feel that he now enjoyed the royal confidence - because shortly thereafter he delivered another bill. Very different to his previous communications, it clearly demonstrated that even if he had not instigated the rebellions, he shared the commons' grievances:

Please it your hyghnes tendirly to considere the grett grutchyng and romore that is unnuversaly in this your reame of that justice is nouthe dewly ministrid to suche as trespass and offende ayens your lawes... Wherfore I your humble sugett and lyge man Richard Duke of York, willyng as effectually as I kan and desiring suerete and prosperite of your most roiall person and welfare of this your noble reame... offer... to execute your commaundements in thes premises of suche offenders and redresse of the seid mysrewlers to my myth and power.[12]

Thus York joined the fold of those accusing Henry's household of malfeasance, thereby implicitly criticising the King himself – a move unlikely to endear him either to the court faction or their royal patrons. Henry's reply may indicate a rare example of shrewdness and clarity, showing him better able to act assertively with people he did not like than with those having greater claim on his emotions. He acknowledged York's offer, 'took on board' the issues, and on the grounds that it was not 'accustumed nor expedient' for him to be advised by a single person, announced he would establish a 'sad and substantial' council to address 'oure gret maters' - and appointed the Duke to sit on it.[13] Alternatively, it could be perceived as rank hypocrisy or woeful self-blindness; given Somerset's level of influence, Henry VI patently *could* be advised by a single voice – provided it was not Richard of York's. Thus the Duke's advice was taken, up to a point, although he did not gain the exclusivity he plainly desired and believed the Beauforts to enjoy. Obliged to accept the situation, he likely felt disappointed and humiliated by Henry's rebuff, and infuriated at the ill-concealed glee no doubt displayed by the household.

As the unrest continued, (Somerset was attacked and robbed in December, narrowly escaping with his life), the threat to his crown apparently galvanised Henry VI into the most decisive phase of his reign. He refused to act on a commons petition to dismiss a number of persons, including Somerset, from his presence; embarked on major judicial progresses to punish miscreants (the first, in Kent, led to the so-called 'Harvest of Heads'); and substantially revised his previous grants for crown lands, which greatly improved the position of the exchequer. York received several offices, including Constable of Rockingham Castle, suggesting that he had not altogether forfeited the royal favour; but he was also re-appointed as Lieutenant of Ireland for ten years[14] which may be construed either as a mark of trust, or a means to get rid of him again. More likely it was the latter, since in May Henry not only rejected a commons petition headed by Thomas Young, one of York's councillors, to recognise the Duke as heir-apparent, but cast Young in the Tower for his presumption.[15] The decay of their relationship is further suggested by events in the summer of 1451, when York intervened to settle a violent dispute between the Earls of Devon and Wiltshire and their respective allies. Henry angrily summoned all parties involved to answer for the disturbances at a council meeting in Coventry, and the Duke, presumably offended at being lumped with the trouble-makers, declined to reply or attend. Matters reached such a pass that in January 1452 a worried York, then at Ludlow, wrote again to the King:

Forasmuch as I, Richard Duke of York, am informed that the king my Sovereign Lord, my heavy lord, is greatly displeased with me, and hath me in distrust by sinister information of mine enemies, adversaries and evil willers, whereas God knoweth from whom nothing is hid, I am and have been and ever will be his true liegeman.[16]

However, being a 'true liegeman' did not equip York with the stomach to endure the King's cronies. Nor they him it seems, for by February he was writing to numerous towns requesting aid to forcibly remove Somerset, whom he blamed for the continuing losses in France - and for continual labours 'about the King's highness for my undoing, and to corrupt my blood, and to disinherit me and my heirs, and such persons as be about me...'[17]

So it was that personal dislike, misunderstanding and mistrust escalated into armed confrontation. Many thousands answered York's call, an indication of popular support and distaste for Beaufort-dominated policies, but more declared for the King. The armies met at Dartford where, unable to prevail by force, York, Lord Cobham and Thomas Courtney, Earl of Devon, knelt before Henry to deliver a lengthy complaint against Somerset. The exercise was fruitless, and probably counter-productive. No matter what arguments were presented or evidence offered, the King would not turn on Edmund Beaufort; the more he was attacked, the more staunchly Henry defended him – and the more his heart hardened against the attackers. Somerset remained in favour while York was escorted ignominiously into London, and obliged to swear an oath of allegiance to King Henry wherein he promised 'never hereafter to make any assembly of your people without your command or licence, or in my lawful defence'.[18] An enforced arbitration between the Dukes, who must by this stage have cordially detested one another, theoretically settled their dispute[19] and in April, York availed himself of a general pardon[20] before retiring to his estates, like as not still angry and embittered.

Although a semblance of order had been restored between his warring magnates, the King's wider problems at home and abroad were far from resolved. In late April 1452, the Duke of Norfolk complained of the 'grettest riots, orryble wrongs and offences done in thise partys by the seide Lord Scales, Thomas Tudenham [steward of the duchy of Norfolk], Mylis Stapleton [and] John Heydon [MP for Norfolk]' while some Norfolk gentlemen including John Paston bemoaned the 'dyvers assaults and ryottes' made by one Charles Nowell.[21] Unrest persisted throughout the year with uprisings in Wales, Shropshire and Kent apparently aimed at replacing the King with York, prompting Henry to undertake further punitive judicial progresses resulting in numerous executions for treason. In the north, the long-running and often violent struggle for dominance between the Percy and Neville families continued, frequently drawing in other noblemen like Thomas, Lord Roos, who sided with the Percys; while in the south-west, the Earl of Devon was still competing with James Butler, Earl of Wiltshire, and waging a private war against William, Baron Bonville. At the same time, King Henry and the Duke of York were both experiencing problems with the same close kinsman, Henry Holland, second Duke of Exeter. Holland was of the Lancastrian royal blood, being the grandson of Elizabeth, sister of Henry IV; he was also York's son-in-law, having been married in 1445 at the age of 15 to the Duke's daughter Anne (then a child of six). Unfortunately, Holland's rank had not endowed him with a ducal income, which may have prompted his ill-advised attempt to fraudulently and forcibly wrest Ampthill Castle from its incumbent, Lord Cromwell, in the summer of 1452 - an avoidable dispute which was to have far wider political consequences in the coming years.[22]

These domestic upheavals notwithstanding, late 1452 and early 1453 were perhaps the zenith of Henry's reign. John Talbot, Earl of Shrewsbury, was enjoying some successes in the re-conquest of Gascony, thanks in part to the assistance of pro-English Bordelais – and finally Queen Margaret had conceived. Meanwhile York was still in disfavour, indicated by a letter from his Duchess to the pregnant Queen. Cecily, as indefatigable a champion of her husband's cause as was Margaret of Henry's, reported that they were both weighed down with heavy sorrow at his estrangement from 'the grace and benevolent favour of that most Christian, most gracious and most merciful prince, the king our sovereign lord', protested his loyalty, and begged the Queen to intercede on their behalf.[23] Margaret's reply, if any, has not survived, although she may not have been pleased by the prospect; following Henry's example she preferred Somerset as her confidant and advisor, automatically putting her at odds with the critical York.

Alas for Henry, his glory days were destined to be few. In July 1453, Shrewsbury's army was destroyed at the Battle of Castillon and the Earl himself killed in the rout; with that, all English possessions save a toe-hold in Calais were effectively lost. This dreadful news, coming atop three years of family strife and serious threats to his crown, may have been the final straw that broke the King's equilibrium and precipitated the mental collapse that proved so fortuitous for York. After years of perceiving himself unfairly treated and ostracised, the Duke could at last claim his due as a prince of the blood, assume his place of primacy on the council – and perhaps most satisfying of all from a personal perspective, revive all his charges against Somerset and commit him to the Tower. In February 1454 came his appointment as King's Lieutenant, and in March, as Protector of the Realm and Chief Councillor, a position consolidated when his brother-in-law Richard Neville, Earl of Salisbury, succeeded as chancellor after the death of Cardinal Kemp.

Trying to restore order to the prevailing climate of anarchy and mayhem was the priority of York's protectorate. He took firm steps to end the Percy-Neville conflict, which had broken out into bloodshed in August 1453 when a party including the Earl of Northumberland's son Thomas Percy, Baron Egremont, attacked the Nevilles at Heworth, near York, on their way back from a family wedding. Predictably, under the circumstances, the Duke resolved their dispute in favour of his Neville in-laws – incidentally putting him at odds with his recalcitrant son-in-law Exeter, who had allied himself with young Percy (an enemy of Lord Cromwell of Ampthill). Exeter's humiliation and alienation from York deepened further when he not only lost his case for Ampthill, but saw Lord Cromwell appointed to Richard's council. His unwise response was to rebel at Spofforth in May 1454, leaving his father-in-law no choice but to quash the uprising and imprison Holland in Pontefract Castle.

York then turned his attentions to making substantial reductions in the vastly expensive royal household. He also, nominally at least, assumed the lieutenancy of Calais, although practically, control remained with Somerset's captains, Rivers and Welles; and his bid for £40,000 to pay the Calais garrison was rejected by parliament, resulting in a mutiny by the unpaid troops. Given time, the Duke might have achieved more at home and abroad, but by late 1454 King Henry was recovering and in early 1455 resumed the reins of government. Unsurprisingly, and no doubt with his wife's full approval, Henry at once set about reversing the protectorate's policies. Infuriatingly for York, the King relieved him of the captaincy of Calais and returned it to Edmund Beaufort, cleared of treason and released from the Tower; and choosing to view their atrocious rift as a purely personal quarrel, subjected their case to arbitration and bound them over to keep the peace to the tune of 20,000 marks. The Duke of Exeter was likewise released from prison, and Salisbury replaced as chancellor by the Archbishop of Canterbury, Thomas Bourchier.

By these actions, Henry VI exacerbated the development of two decidedly opposing factions, and consolidated an alliance between the Duke of York and Earl of Salisbury in defence of their mutual interests. With Somerset back in power and the dire example of Duke Humphrey's destruction fresh in their minds, York and Salisbury must have been in terror for their political futures if not their very lives. Taking up arms may have seemed their only option, especially when the King summoned a great council to the loyalist heartland of Leicester, which they suspected was to indict them of treason or impose other punitive sanctions. Preventing this council was therefore vital, and they set out in force to intercept the royal party at St Albans – like the court faction, still protesting their loyalty and good intentions while accusing the other side of the opposite. In such an atmosphere of accusation and counter-accusation, attempts to reach a peaceful settlement failed and on 22nd May, 1455, battle was joined on St Albans' streets between retinues of the rival magnates, each (whatever their stated justifications) fighting for control of King Henry.

On this occasion, the Yorkists prevailed. Whether by happenstance or deliberate targeting, their bitter enemies Edmund Beaufort, Duke of Somerset, Henry Percy, Earl of Northumberland, and the staunch royal allies Thomas, Lord Clifford and John, Lord Clinton, were all killed. Henry's person duly secured, he was escorted back to London with every semblance of honour. Notwithstanding the shock and grief he must have felt at losing his friends, kinsmen and councillors, at a crown-wearing ceremony on Whitsunday he apparently insisted on receiving his crown from the Duke of York rather than from the archbishop, as was customary. He also permitted the redistribution of key offices including the constableship of England to York, and captaincy of Calais to Salisbury's son Richard Neville, Earl of Warwick; and in a parliamentary pardon dated 24th July 1455, exonerated the

Yorkist lords of blame for St Albans, protected them from retribution and accepted their renewed allegiance.[24]

Do these actions show that Henry VI was tolerant, merciful and infinitely forgiving; cowed into resigning himself to the inevitable; so dazed and distracted by bereavement and a slight wound sustained at St Albans that he would consent to anything; or did he now truly believe that the Beauforts and others were guilty as charged? Certainly the astonishing *volte-face* lends credence to the Duke's conviction that Henry had indeed been poisoned against him – the moment Somerset's influence was removed York could step into the vacuum, persuade Henry of his good faith and effect a reconciliation. If so, it is further evidence of the King's chameleonic opinions which changed colour depending on whom he stood next to; that the opposing factions fully grasped this weakness explains why they fought so viciously to possess him.

Henry VI was now under the 'care' of the Yorkists. Possibly these violent upheavals, coming so soon after his return to health, precipitated a second (albeit less serious) bout of mental illness because by late summer or autumn, York was once again acting as Protector.[25] Thus ostensibly, St Albans and its aftermath had strengthened his position; by permanently removing Somerset and Northumberland, the Duke (and many others) must have hoped that a more settled and equitable government would ensue. And so it appeared until early 1456, when parliamentary divisions arose regarding a controversial act of resumption, supported by York and the commons but rejected by most of the lords. King Henry, whose health must have significantly improved, was called in to make a final decision. He opted to reserve his prerogative, make exemptions to the act and revoke the protectorate (or York may have resigned). But the Duke was still in favour, remaining principal councillor and lieutenant in which capacity his next move was to Sandal Castle - a convenient base for operations against James II of Scotland, who had declared war, moved into Northumberland, and ironically, offered Richard support in claiming the English throne.[26]

With York's withdrawal from court, the weathervane swung back. Queen Margaret bitterly blamed him for a great many things including Somerset's death, sundry rebellions against royal authority, the curtailment of their household, and the thwarting of her hopes for the regency. Described in February 1456 as 'a grete and stronge laboured woman [who] spareth no peyne to sue hire thinges to an intent and conclusion to hir power',[27] Margaret took advantage of the Duke's absence and persuaded Henry to remove his court to the midlands – possibly in part due to the unrest stirring again in London and Kent. This was followed by an alarming outburst of trouble caused by two of York's tenants, Sir Walter Devereux and Sir William Herbert: in August, while the Duke was occupied defending the northern borders against Scottish incursions, they marched into Wales, seized the castles at Aberystwyth and Carmarthen, (nominally York's possessions, but garrisoned by supporters of Somerset who refused to submit to his authority), and imprisoned the King's half-brother Edmund Tudor, Earl of Richmond. This inevitably fed Lancastrian paranoia and the suspicion of York's complicity; accordingly the King and Queen repaired to the freshly-fortified Kenilworth Castle and thereafter maintained their court primarily at Coventry.

So the lasting legacy of St Albans was a resurgence of anti-Yorkist feeling, especially among the sons of Lancastrian nobles slain there. In September, the Duke was subjected to the unpleasant spectacle of five dog heads, bearing scurrilous verses against him in their jaws, impaled on stakes outside his London lodgings.[28] Meanwhile Queen Margaret seems to have been dictating royal policy in a manner not universally welcomed. At a great council meeting in October where York stood 'in right good conceyt with the Kyng, but not in gret conceyt with the Quene', Thomas Bourchier, Archbishop of Canterbury, and Henry, Viscount Bourchier, were respectively replaced as chancellor and treasurer by William Waynflete, Bishop of Winchester, and John Talbot, second Earl of Shrewsbury. The Duke of Buckingham, (the Bourchiers' half-brother), who intervened to ensure that York was not 'distressed in his departyng', also took it 'right straungely that bothe his brethren are so sodeynly discharged from ther offices.'[29] After the political came physical attacks: in November, Warwick was ambushed by Shrewsbury, Exeter and Henry Beaufort, the vengeful new Duke of Somerset, who soon after also attacked the Duke of York in Coventry.

Consequently, 1457 was an uneasy year. Devereux and Herbert were punished harshly for their insurrection; York's enemies could produce no convincing evidence of his involvement, but the government's fear of further unrest in the shires is demonstrated by the appointment of 14 magnates (not including York, Warwick or Salisbury) to resist and suppress rebels in counties around Kenilworth and Coventry.[30] Despite the open antagonism now being displayed by his wife and her adherents, Henry VI remained hopeful that the divisions could be resolved peacefully, and in October, called a great council aimed at setting apart 'such variances as be betwixt divers lords'. His hopes were laudable if somewhat naïve - before a second such meeting in January 1458, the disgruntled Exeter, his friend Egremont and John, the new Lord Clifford, tried to ambush York and Warwick as they rode to Westminster; Somerset and Henry Percy, third Earl of Northumberland, made another attempt on Warwick two months later.

Henry persisted nonetheless. His solution was reasonable enough, on the face of it, although it backtracked from his earlier position. Now the Yorkists were to atone for the deaths at St Albans by founding a chantry at the abbey, paying £45 per year for masses to be said there, and making financial restitution to the bereaved. The lords were obliged to accept arbitration and take part in the so-called 'Loveday' at St Paul's, a great public parade of reconciliation where Somerset walked with Salisbury and Exeter with Warwick. Tellingly, behind King Henry came Richard of York, hand-in-hand not with a noble St Albans widow but with Queen Margaret. A commendable endeavour on the King's part, it must have been reassuring to a populace subjected for months to the aggressive posturing of the magnates' respective retinues; but alas for Henry's good intentions, there could be no such cheap pay-off for the corrosive personal scores that by now existed.

Henry's itinerary after Loveday suggests that he was withdrawing from state affairs, (as had been his tendency since St Albans), spending more time at his beloved abbeys and priories or residing with the Queen. Meanwhile there were renewed peace initiatives with France - even as the fragile Loveday accord broke down, as demonstrated by an assassination attempt on the Earl of Warwick variously dated to late 1458 or early 1459. Revived worries about Henry's security are also evinced by the order of pikes and clubs for the royal household in December 1458.[31]

The situation continued to deteriorate during 1459, possibly due to Queen Margaret's increasing dominance, as contemporary chronicles suggest: 'no lord of England at this time dare disobey the queen, for she ruled all that was done about the king'.[32] (Any notion of a queen ruling through her enfeebled husband was of course anathema to 15th century male commentators. Margaret herself may have relished the power, believed that she was entitled to exercise it, or simply felt that under the circumstances of Henry's inertia she had little choice). Given the Yorkist or Lancastrian bias of the chronicles it is difficult to ascertain precisely what lay behind the increasing tensions of that year, although according to the *English Chronicle*, '...the queen, with such as were of her affinity, ruled the realm as she liked, gathering riches innumerable. The officers of the realm, especially the Earl of Wiltshire, treasurer of England, to enrich himself, fleeced the poor people, disinherited rightful heirs and did many wrongs.'[33] This implies a recurrence of the dangerous conditions that had led to Cade's rebellion and brought York 'on board' as a critic of the government and champion of reform; Warwick's growing ascendancy in Calais may also have given cause for concern. Moreover, unwelcome allegations were being bruited about that Prince Edward was not Henry's true son but 'a bastard conceived in adultery', while Polydore Vergil reports on the extreme bad blood between the noble factions - the 'mutual rehearsal of old injuries, and quarrelous repetition as well of late as of almost forgotten faults' - and that Somerset and Buckingham had convinced the Queen of 'a malignant enterprise whereby the Duke of York [might] attain the sovereignty.'[34]

In response to these threats real, imagined or manufactured, the Lancastrians began preparing for war. Queen Margaret, presumably terrified and desperate to protect her son's inheritance, allegedly tried to persuade Henry to abdicate in the prince's favour, distributing the Lancastrian swan livery to the nobility of Cheshire and elsewhere to secure their support. If this is true it suggests that she tacitly acknowledged her husband's failings, and hoped that loyalists and disaffected subjects alike would rally behind another Lancastrian-dominated minority rather than see York on the throne. It is hard to believe that this would have helped, and in any case, Henry would not go. In April, he sent privy seal documents to John Paston and his son, among many others, instructing them to be 'wyth the Kyngg at Leycester the x. day of May, with as many personys defensebylly arayid as they myte according to ther degree, and… expensys for ii. monthis.'[35] In May the court repaired to the safety of Kenilworth and Coventry, where bow-staves and arrows sufficient for 3,000 archers were ordered; and in June, ominously for the Yorkists, a great council was called. The Bourchiers, York, the Earls of Salisbury, Warwick and Arundel, and the Bishops of Exeter and Ely were all summoned, but presumably fearing for their safety, chose not to attend.

Whether this was planned in advance or resulted (as the Lancastrians claimed) from their non-attendance, all were indicted in absentia of treason, allegedly at Queen Margaret's instigation. Maurer suggests that these indictments amounted to little more than 'a slap on the wrist for non-attendance', and expresses scepticism regarding the Queen's level of influence on proceedings.[36] But even without her active intervention, Margaret's presence - beautiful, tragically beset by worries for her husband and son, and united in grief with the bereaved of St Albans – would have had considerable impact on her supporters, bringing to the fore all their gallant instincts and loathing of the Yorkist lords responsible.

Whatever the rest may have thought, the indictments were plainly more than a slap on the wrist from the perspective of York, Warwick and Salisbury. They began mustering troops, resolving to meet up at York's town of Ludlow and 'journey to the king' either, (as they claimed), to peacefully plead their cause[37] or, (as the Lancastrians claimed), to 'falsely and traitorously raise war.'[38] The Queen's affinity, equally fearing a successful *coup* or that Henry would once again cave in and grant pardons, were similarly resolved to prevent them doing so. Bloodshed ensued on 23rd September when Lancastrian forces from Cheshire and Shropshire, under the command of Lord Audley, intercepted the Earl of Salisbury at Blore Heath. Audley was killed in the encounter, his men routed, and the Earl proceeded without further hindrance to meet York at Ludlow, where they were shortly joined by Warwick with a contingent of Calais veterans. The lords went together to Worcester cathedral, where they vowed allegiance to the King in the presence of witnesses. They then wrote to Henry pledging their good faith, and complaining that their lordships and tenants had been robbed and despoiled due to the malice of his household men[39] before repairing to Ludford Bridge, just south of Ludlow, where their combined army was entrenched.

Large Lancastrian forces were also converging on Ludford Bridge. Among them was King Henry himself, whose presence undoubtedly brought men flocking to his banner and caused qualms in the Yorkist ranks, while loudly proclaimed offers of a general pardon further lessened their stomach for the fight. Warwick summarily rejected the pardon on behalf of the Yorkist lords, on the grounds that those they had received after St Albans had proved useless; however, it was accepted by the seasoned warrior Andrew Trollope, who led the Calais troops to defect. Yorkist morale drooped, desertions increased and heavily outnumbered,

York and his commanders recognised the hopelessness of their position. Rather than have their army (and like as not, themselves) slaughtered to no purpose, they trusted in the royal pardon to spare the rank-and-file and abandoned the field. Travelling in two groups to increase their chances of evading capture or shipwreck, Richard and his second son Edmund, Earl of Rutland, fled to Ireland while Warwick, Salisbury and York's eldest son Edward, Earl of March, fetched up in Calais; they may also have embarked for Ireland, but changed their plans after being blown off course.[40]

Baulked of decisive victory, the Lancastrians plundered York's town and castle of Ludlow, raiding the taverns, despoiling women, and leaving the Duchess of York no choice but to throw herself on the King's mercy. She and her younger children were 'taken to the Duke of Buckingham and his lady [Cecily's sister] and there she was till the field was done at Northampton, and she was kept full strait with many a great rebuke' on account of her husband's conduct.[41] In December 1459, the unfortunate Duchess was obliged to listen while Richard, her two eldest sons and their allies were attainted and stripped of all their estates, honours and dignities. Meanwhile in Ireland, the Duke was planning his next move...

Plate 6: Stained glass window from Trinity College Library, showing the Duke of York in armour. Photo by Les Goodey; reproduced by kind permission of the Master and Fellows, Trinity College, Cambridge.

York's Claim to the Throne

What could York do, faced with such perilous choices? Remaining a fugitive and abandoning his beloved Duchess and children to their fate was not an option any honourable prince could consider. Accepting defeat was no more attractive. To return humbly, endeavour to make peace with his opponents and submit to whatever punishment they meted out could easily result in his exile, imprisonment or execution. Even if he survived, the one thing he could not do was change his pedigree and legitimate claim to the crown; so his position and safety, and that of his family, could never be assured. The King's trust and favour were too precarious and his enemies too potent – he had no guarantee that they would not continue to work against him and ultimately destroy him as they had Humphrey of Gloucester. Possibly he could return in force and reclaim control of King Henry; if successful, in the short-term his enemies would be politically neutralised in a repetition of his protectorates or events after St Albans. Or he could try for a more radical and permanent solution: to rid England of the Lancastrian liability and assume the mantle of monarch himself.

With one or both of the latter objectives in mind, the Yorkist lords in exile launched a propaganda campaign, exploiting the dissatisfaction felt with the current regime particularly in the south-east. They issued from Calais a widely-publicised list of grievances with which many could identify, including the loss of France despite heavy taxation imposed for its defence, the corruption of Henry's household men, Humphrey of Gloucester's murder, and their own unlawful attainder. As was politic, (and may conceivably have been true), their manifesto reiterated the tale told since Jack Cade's day: that their complaints were not against the King, to whom they remained loyal, but against the evil counsellors responsible for all these ills - namely their 'mortal and extreme enemies', Viscount Beaumont and the Earls of Wiltshire and Shrewsbury.[42] York's feelings towards Wiltshire may have been particularly bitter, since the Earl had been a former ally and annuitant until 1452, when he began inclining towards Somerset and the Queen's faction – and reaping rich reward.

By summer 1460 the ground was prepared. Warwick's party, among them the papal legate Francesco Coppini, landed at Sandwich on 26th June aided by Lord Fauconberg, Archbishop Bourchier and William Neville. With their ranks swelled by disaffected Kentishmen, they marched on London where only the Tower resisted their entry; and leaving Salisbury in charge of the capital, struck north to find the King. On 10th July they encountered the royal forces at Northampton and embarked upon the customary parleys to gain peaceful access to Henry's presence. This failing, battle was joined (according to the *English Chronicle*, in a heavy rain that rendered the King's ordnance useless) and the Yorkists won the day. Among those slain were their despised enemies Beaumont, Shrewsbury, Buckingham and

Egremont. The Earl of Wiltshire, the treasurer Waynflete and Laurence Booth, Keeper of the Privy Seal, all escaped, but the hapless King was captured in his tent.

What followed was predictable: all honour was shown to Henry even as his authority was undermined and his adherents stripped of office. Warwick's brother George, Bishop of Exeter, became chancellor; the Bishop of Bath, Robert Stillington, replaced Booth as Privy Seal; Viscount Bourchier was made treasurer; and a parliament was called, to which the Duke of York and Earl of March were summoned.[43]

Meanwhile York's Irish supporters were obtaining parliamentary licences to leave for England, and the Duke was reaching a fateful conclusion. No longer would he permit his prospects to hang on King Henry's fragile regard, ever vulnerable to the malicious tongues of his favourites. Henry simply did not like York well enough to accept his exclusive counsel; so if he could not safeguard his position by ruling *through* the King, all that remained was to rule *instead*. The Duke must press his own claim to the throne, and his renunciation of allegiance to Henry VI can be construed from his letters of September 1460, dated only by the year of grace, not the regnal year; there is also a chronicle reference to York starting to bear the whole arms of England at this time.[44]

The Duke landed near Chester around 9th September, whereupon Warwick paid him a four-day visit no doubt to discuss the forthcoming parliament - and other pressing matters. York's decision cannot have occasioned shock or dismay - according to Francesco Coppini, the Earl had called Henry 'a dolt and a fool', and said that 'the Duke of York… would now be on the throne if there were any regard to justice.'[45] (That York was confident of Warwick's approval, and trusted him to whip up support in advance, is further indicated by the regal nature of his subsequent entry into London). After their meeting, York moved on to Ludlow where local gentry invited him to assume the throne[46] - an understandable response since the ransacking in 1459 had left anti-Lancastrian sentiments running high. From Ludlow the Duke followed a circuitous route to the capital via his estates in Shrewsbury, Hereford, Gloucester and Abingdon, reassuring his tenants and recruiting support as he went; and reaching London on 10th October while parliament was in session, made the biggest gamble of his career.

This momentous occasion is recorded in several contemporary accounts.[47] York entered the city with great pomp, his sword borne before him like a king, marched into Westminster Hall and laid his hand on the throne. By this stage his own views were deeply entrenched, and perhaps reinforced by the reactions he had encountered *en route* to London: Henry VI had repeatedly shown himself unfit to rule, a weak-minded subject of corrupt, incompetent councillors who between them had oppressed the populace, ruined England and lost France.[48] Looking back on the reign it is easy to agree with the Duke's conclusion, as did many people at the time. Convinced of his rectitude, his lawful claim and his ability to do better than Henry, York believed the majority of his peers would agree. After all, what sane man would prefer continued misrule by a Lancastrian sheep to a sensible Yorkist government with a proven warrior and administrator at its head? Confidently, he awaited acclamation; it must have been a hideous shock when he was greeted instead by confused consternation.

Why was the expected relief and approbation not forthcoming? York was popular as a 'good lord', champion of reform and defender of the commons' interests. However, it was not the people who made kings but the nobility, among whom he had bitter enemies. These included his son-in-law, Exeter, whose ambitions York had thwarted; Thomas Courtney, the new Earl of Devon and a staunch Lancastrian by virtue of his marriage to Queen Margaret's cousin Marie; and the sons of lords slain at St Albans. Besides, all the nobility, friend or foe, had sworn oaths to uphold Henry VI as their sovereign - vows taken far more seriously than in our present secular age. The most genuinely devout would have baulked at imperilling their souls by breaking such an oath, and been appalled by the Yorkists' own oath-breaking; the timid may have felt 'better the devil you know'; the cynical, especially Lancastrians, would have realised their interests were far better served by a puppet king than they necessarily would be by the more rigorous and capable York. Some may have disliked him personally, perhaps believing he had initiated a decade of unrest purely for his own advantage, and resented this attempt at a *fait accompli*; or feared (with good reason) that his dynastic claim would not end England's problems. Perhaps such a radical challenge was simply too much, too soon, for conservatives and wavering supporters of King Henry to cope with. Altogether, the risk was too great - if York's bid failed, those who sided with him could be attainted and lose everything, up to and including their lives.

York had no choice but to brazen it out. Taking up residence in the royal apartments, he stood by his claim and obliged parliament to investigate, protesting 'that he would no longer endure the injustices which the three Henrys, the usurpers, had for so long inflicted on his line.'[49] The complex buck of rightful inheritance from Edward III was passed back and forth between lords, lawyers and King until finally, on 25th October, Chancellor Neville presented a compromise akin to the Treaty of Troyes: Henry VI would continue to rule until his death, whereupon the crown would pass to Richard of York or his heirs instead of the Lancastrian Prince of Wales. Under this 'Act of Accord', the Duke and his sons reaffirmed their allegiance to King Henry, who in turn was bound by indenture to keep the agreement.[50] The attainders issued after Ludford Bridge were repealed and York was confirmed as heir-apparent, given the protection of the law of treason, and received the requisite titles and endowments including the principality of Wales.

The Duke had to content himself with this partial success. His claim had been comprehensively examined and officially validated, albeit his reign would be deferred and being ten years older than Henry, he might never live to see it. But for the present, his exalted state was finally recognised and he was monarch in all but name; Henry VI was virtually a prisoner, and in the absence of his wife and usual councillors, had no will – or option - but to accede to Yorkist demands.

If the Lancastrians had lacked a figurehead, matters *might* have gone well enough for the king-in-waiting; possibly the nobles bereaved at St Albans and Blore Heath would have resigned themselves to the new regime rather than risk attainder, if a lesser woman than Margaret of Anjou had meekly accepted her fate. But Margaret was no ordinary medieval queen - far from it - and outrage now compelled this 'great and strong laboured woman' to a decidedly unconventional course: to take up the banner herself.

On hearing news of events at Northampton, she had immediately fled to Wales and thence to Scotland with the young prince, and set about recruiting aid to oppose the Yorkists. Thus preparations to 'liberate' Henry VI probably began even before the outcome of the October parliament was known, and when the Act of Accord was broadcast they took on far greater urgency. Understandably, the Act was 'detestable and accursed'[51] to Margaret; it stripped her son of his rightful inheritance, and when Henry died she would lose all the power and prestige she could otherwise expect to enjoy. Her honour had also been impugned, and failure to act would be tantamount to admitting there was truth in the rumour - that Prince Edward was a bastard with no rights worth defending. She also knew that what Henry had been persuaded into, she could just as easily persuade him out of, given chance. It was therefore imperative to regain control of the King, restore the old order and overturn the Act of Accord – ideally by snuffing out York and his heirs on the battlefield - even though by Henry's newly-passed law, Margaret and her followers became rebels and traitors. But they cared little for the risk of attainders when passive acceptance would cost them far more. Besides, they viewed it as fighting *for* Henry, not against him; theirs was not rebellion, but rescue. In their eyes, York was the real traitor – and it would take his death and the destruction of his House before the Lancastrian monarchy could be secure.

So throughout the autumn of 1460, Queen Margaret wrote to her stalwarts including the Dukes of Somerset and Exeter, the Earls of Devon and Northumberland, and the Lords Roos, Clifford and Dacre, bidding them to raise troops – an order they must have gladly obeyed, the Act of Accord being equally repugnant to them. Whether the Lancastrian mustering point was York, Hull or Pontefract is a matter of conjecture. Feasibly, Hull could have been the initial muster point for troops travelling by sea from the east coast or Scotland, where their presence would have prevented the Yorkists from using the port; however, this view (based on a single reference in *Gregory's Chronicle*) has recently been challenged.[52] Whatever the case, both towns are conveniently located for a march to Pontefract, an obvious choice for the main muster: a major royal castle in a region of strength, centrally situated for the converging armies and safely distant from York's south-eastern power base. Northumberland must have been delighted by this excuse to revive hostilities against his old adversaries, the pro-Yorkist branch of the Nevilles. His vengeful companions were doubtless just as glad to ravage the northern estates held by Salisbury and York, conveniently combining personal gratification with a plan to bring the Duke to battle on ground of their choosing.

Neither the widespread movement of thousands of men nor this campaign of harassment could remain secret for long. Now it was both York's duty as a good lord to protect his own tenants, and his duty as King's Lieutenant to suppress such insurrections. Accordingly, in November 1460 Henry's 'derrest cousyn Richard… rightfull heire of the Reaumes of Englond and Fraunce and of the Lordship and Land of Ireland' undertook to 'represse, subdue and appese' the said 'rebellions, murders, riottes, spoiling, extorsions and oppressions', with the full authority granted by Parliament.[53] No doubt some members speculated, possibly even hoped, that his mission would prove fatal. Given that he made out his will before departing, the thought had plainly crossed Richard's mind too.[54]

Some historians suggest that York's preparations for the campaign were sluggish and ill-made and that he failed to comprehend the magnitude of the task that lay ahead[55] - but this is perhaps to underestimate the logistical difficulties he faced at that time. The Duke and his allies were obliged to spend November wrestling with issues of manpower and finance, and juggling resources to control Calais as well as dealing with the widespread problems at home. The Yorkist forces accordingly divided: the Earl of March was dispatched to Shrewsbury to prevent Jasper Tudor from joining the Queen's army before reinforcing his father in Yorkshire; the Earl of Warwick would stay behind to guard the King and capital; and the key mission of quelling the northern rebellions naturally fell to York, supported by his younger son the Earl of Rutland, and the Earl of Salisbury, whose estates were also under attack. By December their strategy was in place; and as the Duke departed for Wakefield, so we depart from comparatively well-documented history into the realm of speculation and myth.

In conclusion, Richard of York initially respected and served Henry VI as his sovereign, however much he may have privately despised or despaired of his weakness as a man. As the Duke consistently claimed, his paramount concerns may well have been the good of both King and country - but he could never abide Henry's favoured household men, rightly or wrongly regarding them as incompetent, treacherous and corrupt; they in turn viewed him in exactly the same jaundiced light. The King's lack of objectivity and failure to manage his nobility gave rise to flagrant abuses of the law, uncontrolled local feuding and impossibly adversarial conditions wherein one magnate, or clique, could only prosper at direct cost to another. It was an environment guaranteed to foster jealousy and resentment, and the more York accused, complained and defended himself from attack, the more he was disliked, distrusted and seen as a trouble-maker. St Albans probably marked the turning point from resolvable argument to bloody vendetta;

the deaths of York's rivals spawned a new generation bent on revenge, made an implacable foe of Queen Margaret, and drove history into a repetitive cycle. Two weak kings had already lost their crowns by alienating their established nobility, and Richard's own father had rebelled against a monarch whose treatment he found intolerable. Now York, whose service had failed to win the regard of his sovereign, found himself in the same situation. His response was to press his own claim to rule – whereby the last fatal chain of events was set into motion.

Notes

1. Johnson, *op cit*, p. 78.
2. Impeachment of the Duke of Suffolk in Gairdner, *op cit*, pp. 99 – 105.
3. Wolffe, *op cit*, pp. 221 – 229.
4. William Lomner to John Paston, 5th May 1450, in Gairdner, *op cit*, pp. 124 – 126.
5. The final lines of the 'Warning to King Henry', quoted in Wolffe, *op cit*, p.229.
6. Johnson, *op cit*, p. 79.
7. From various sources quoted in 'Duke Richard of York's Intentions in 1450', Griffiths, *op cit*, p.282.
8. Wolffe, *op cit*, pp. 234 – 236. According to the *English Chronicle*, *op cit*, p.65, one such traitor the Kentishmen cried out against was Lord Say, the King's Chamberlain, who was committed to the Tower.
9. Johnson, *op cit*, pp. 80 – 81.
10. Griffiths, *op cit*, pp. 299 – 300. The correspondence between the Duke and King is derived from the Beverley Corporation Archives 'Town Chartulary'.
11. From King Henry's reply to York's letters, *ibid*, p. 301.
12. *Ibid*, p. 302.
13. *Ibid*, pp. 303 – 304.
14. Postlethwaite, *op cit*, p. 19.
15. *Annales Rerum Anglicarum*, reproduced in *Letters And Papers Illustrative of the Wars of the English in France*, J.S. Stevenson (ed.), 1864, pp. 769 – 770, and quoted in Dockray, *op cit*, 2000, pp. 57 – 58. The *Annales* are sometimes attributed to the 15th century antiquary William of Worcester, but this is unlikely to be correct.
16. Postlethwaite, *op cit*, p. 20.
17. From York's manifesto to the burgesses of Shrewsbury, quoted in Dockray, *op cit*, 2000, pp. 59 – 60.
18. *Ibid*, pp. 60 – 61.
19. Postlethwaite, *op cit*, p. 20; Johnson, *op cit*, p. 117.

20. Wolffe, *op cit*, p. 256.
21. Some gentlemen of Norfolk to the sheriff; John Paston to the sheriff, both 23rd April 1452, in Gairdner, *op cit*, p. 230 – 233.
22. Michael Hicks, 'Holland, Henry, second duke of Exeter (1430–1475)', *Oxford Dictionary of National Biography*, Oxford University Press, on-line edition, 2004.
23. The Duchess of York's letter is reproduced fully in *Letters of Medieval Women*, ed. Anne Crawford, Sutton Publishing, 2002, pp. 233 – 235.
24. From the parliamentary rolls quoted in Dockray, *op cit*, 2000, p. 73.
25. *Benet's Chronicle* dates the second protectorate to July 1455; the *Chancery Patent Rolls* place York's appointment in November – see Dockray, *op cit*, 2000, p. 67 and p. 74.
26. Wolffe, *op cit*, p. 302.
27. John Bocking to Sir John Fastolf in Gairdner, *op cit*, p.378.
28. Johnson, *op cit*, pp. 176 – 177.
29. Quotes from James Gresham to John Paston, 16th October 1456, in Gairdner, *op cit*, pp. 407 – 408.
30. Wolffe, *op cit*, p. 310.
31. *Ibid*, pp. 313 – 316.
32. *Brut or Chronicles of England*, ed. F.W.D. Brie, 1908, pp. 526 – 527.
33. *English Chronicle*, *op cit*, pp. 79 – 80.
34. Vergil, *op cit*, pp. 101 - 102.
35. An anxious-sounding Margaret Paston to her husband John on 29th April 1459, in Gairdner, *op cit*, p.438.
36. Maurer, *op cit*, pp. 164 – 165.
37. Statement by Earl of Warwick from *Whethamsted's Register*, H.T. Riley (ed.), Vol. 1, 1872, pp. 339 – 341; quoted in Dockray, *op cit*, 2000, pp. 82 – 83.
38. Proceedings of Coventry parliament, Dockray, *op cit*, 2000, p. 83.
39. The Yorkist lords' letter to Henry VI is given in the *English Chronicle*, *op cit*, pp. 81 – 83.
40. Johnson, *op cit*, pp. 194 – 195.
41. *Chronicle of William Gregory*, *op cit*, pp. 206 – 207.
42. Johnson, *op cit*, pp. 201 – 203. A full account of the Duke and Earls' articles bemoaning the state of the nation, the murder of Humphrey of Gloucester and alleged attempt to murder York appears in the *English Chronicle*, *op cit*, pp. 86 – 90.
43. Johnson, *op cit*, p. 207.
44. Wolffe, *op cit*, p. 323, quoting K.B. McFarlane, 'The Wars of the Roses', *Proceedings of the British Academy*, 1965, 93, and the *Chronicle of William Gregory*, *op cit*, p. 208.
45. Maurer, *op cit*, p.176.

46. Johnson, *op cit,* p.212.

47. See Dockray, *op cit*, 2000, pp. 92 – 100.

48. While he had publicly accepted and supported Henry as monarch, York's private feelings may have been very different; according to Polydore Vergil, the Duke considered the King 'a man of soft and feeble spirit, of little wit, and unmeet in all respects for the right government of a commonwealth', Vergil, *op cit*, p. 94.

49. *Crowland Chronicle Continuations 1459 – 1486*, N. Pronay and J. Cox (eds.), Richard III and Yorkist History Trust, Allan Sutton Publishing, 1986, p. 111.

50. Parliamentary Rolls, quoted in Haigh, *op cit*, p. 130.

51. *Crowland Chronicle Continuations*, *op cit*, p. 113.

52. See Haigh, *op cit*, p. 14, for a summary of the arguments. A rejection of Hull as the muster point is given by Audrey Howe in 'The Road to Wakefield: Winter 1460 Part Two', *Blanc Sanglier* (magazine of the Yorkshire Branch of the Richard III Society), Vol. 43, No. 3, August 2009, pp. 15 – 18.

53. Parliamentary Rolls, quoted in Haigh, *op cit*, pp. 131 – 132.

54. Johnson, *op cit,* p. 221.

55. *Ibid,* p. 222; Michael D. Miller, *Wars of the Roses*, on-line version, 2003, Chapter 52, p. 2, calls the Yorkist assembly 'leisurely' and 'casual', and the march north 'carelessly conducted.'

CHAPTER 3: DISPELLING THE MYTHS

We know that York's company left London in December 1460, marched to Sandal Castle and were defeated in battle at Wakefield, but there is very little flesh on the bones of these facts. Even the date he set out is disputed: Vitellius' *Chronicles of London* and the *Great Chronicle of London* say December 2nd; John Benet gives the 5th; *Gregory's Chronicle* the 9th and its anonymous continuation, December 11th. Similar uncertainty exists regarding the Duke's provision of men and arms: the *Annales Rerum Anglicarum* credits him with 'many thousands' and *Whethamsted's Register* with 'a great ordinance of guns and other stuffs of war', while the *English Chronicle* gives him only 'a few persons'.

Maybe the reality falls somewhere between. The necessary division of Yorkist forces may have given the Duke fewer troops than he would have liked for the northern campaign, and obliged him to recruit more along the way. Nonetheless, the retinues of three major magnates would have amounted to hundreds if not thousands of men, not counting York's contingent from Ireland and the many disaffected south-easterners who must have gladly answered his call to arms; and with the Tower of London's arsenal at his disposal it should have been a well-arrayed and provisioned army that set out from the capital.

Their departure date was probably earlier rather than later, given that the march alone (of nearly 200 miles) could have taken around ten days, not counting delays *en route* to muster additional troops. So if the Yorkists left London in the first week of December and arrived at Sandal Castle before Christmas, they were not exactly dawdling - especially considering the season. Medieval campaigns usually took place in summer, when milder weather and better road conditions made it easier to move, feed and keep troops healthy in the field. This atypical winter campaign reflected the critical times, and the Yorkist march may have been slowed by wet, muddy roads, flooded river fords and the extra weight of sodden equipment. Heavy guns may have further hampered their progress, and it has been suggested that the artillery train was forced to turn back by the state of the roads.[1] Haigh believes this is borne out because 'no artillery was involved in the battle of Wakefield'[2] - although absence of evidence is not proof of absence, particularly when the documentary sources are limited and highly selective in what they record, and no systematic archaeological investigation has taken place on the battlefield. Moreover, the 15th century economy did not permit England's road network (based on Roman roads, later tracks and hollow-ways) to become impassable for the cold months; trade, commerce, administration, ecclesiastical and state business went on as usual. The nobility moved around managing their estates, and the itineraries of medieval monarchs clearly show that they (together with their households, baggage trains, hundreds of staff and horses) could, and did, travel extensively during the winter, typically covering around 20 miles a day.[3] So while the Yorkist advance *may* have been slowed by poor weather and roads, the possibility that they arrived at Sandal Castle with an intact artillery train should not be discounted.

No record exists of York's intentions at this stage; his battle plan, destination and precise itinerary are all unknown. One clue in the *Annales Rerum Anglicarum* (see below) suggests he may originally have been bound for the northern capital of York – in which case he probably took the direct route up the Great North Road, halting at towns like Peterborough, Huntingdon and Newark to gather men and supplies (see Fig. 1). Salisbury and Rutland may have followed slightly different paths; *Whethamsted's Register* says that the Yorkist lords journeyed separately to make it easier to find places to stay (implying that their numbers were substantial). Indeed, it makes sense if they had fanned out from the main road to maximise their trawl of troops along the way, although if this was the case, the point at which they rejoined forces is unknown.

On nearing Yorkshire, the Duke presumably discovered that the Lancastrians were holding Pontefract Castle in strength, which would explain his decision to leave the main road and strike off north-west for his town of Wakefield, a suitable place to confront them. With his destination fixed and maybe 30 miles left to travel, it is likely that an advance party was dispatched to warn Sandal Castle of the army's impending arrival, and/or to seek supplies and accommodation for an interim halt at Worksop. Thereafter Richard's intention may have been to continue his journey via his castle at Conisbrough, then along the Roman roads to approach Sandal from the south-east.

In the meantime, the Duke of Somerset was hastening up from his castle at Corfe on the Isle of Purbeck in Dorset to join his allies at Pontefract; according to *Gregory's Chronicle* he came with the Earl of Devon via Bath, Cirencester, Evesham and Coventry. The *English Chronicle* credits them with 800 men, a relatively small, mobile contingent which may then have travelled to Leicester in the Lancastrian heartlands, and on via Nottingham and Mansfield to approach Worksop from the south-west. But whichever route they took, it inadvertently placed them on a collision course with the advancing Yorkists, giving rise to the first mystery of the Wakefield campaign:

The Myth of the Vanquished Vanguard

If historians refer to the Worksop incident at all, it is usually to illustrate York's military ineptitude in allowing his vanguard to blunder into Somerset's army and be cut to pieces. This interpretation rests on a single report in the *Annales Rerum Anglicarum*, a frequently-quoted version of which says:

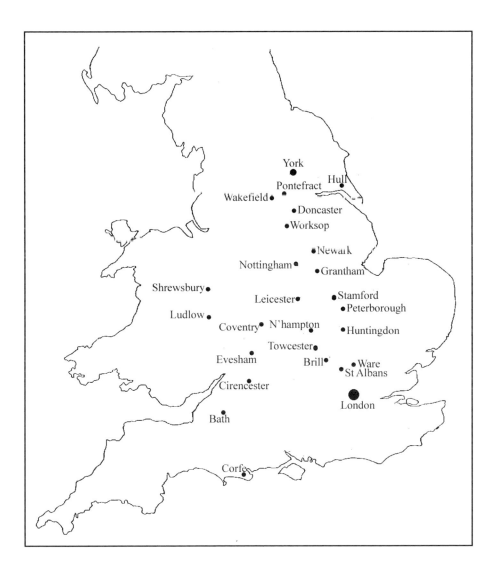

Figure 1: Known or conjectured stages on the journeys north in December 1460. York, Rutland and Salisbury headed NNW from London, probably following or parallel to the Great North Road; the Earl of March travelled NW to Shrewsbury, possibly via Brill and Towcester; Somerset and Devon went NE to Pontefract via Bath, Cirencester, Evesham, Coventry and Worksop.

> *Parliament being prorogued in December, the duke and earl* [ie York and Salisbury] *hastened from London with a large armed force towards York, but coming unexpectedly upon troops of the Duke of Somerset at Worksop, their vanguard was destroyed.*[4]

Taken at face value, it seems strange that so important an event as the loss of a whole vanguard should leave so little trace in the historical record. Yet while other chroniclers refer to the depletion of York's army at Wakefield by foragers, they make no mention of depletion due to the loss of his vanguard at Worksop - suggesting that they either did not know about it, or considered it too trivial to report. This seems odd, to say the least; but the original Latin text tells a rather different story:

> *Et mensis Decembris* [gap in ms] *parliamentum adjornatur. Et dux Eboraci cum comite Sarum, et aliis multis armatis, de Londone versus Eboracum tetenderunt, ubi praeeuntes sui ad numerum 3*[gap in ms] *per gentes ducis Somercetiae interimuntur apud Worsop.*

Literally translated, this means: 'And on [day missing] of the month of December Parliament was adjourned. And the duke of York, with the earl of Salisbury and many thousand other armed men went [lit. 'stretched', an evocative term for a large force] from London towards York, when his goers-before [lit.], to the number of 3[...], were cut off by the people of the duke of Somerset at Worksop.'[5]

What does this tell us? In the generally-accepted version, these 'goers-before' are construed as York's whole vanguard, whereas in the more ambiguous Latin they could equally be a smaller group of outriders, a scouting party, or even messengers sent to prepare Sandal Castle to receive the Yorkist army. It is deeply unfortunate that an area of damage occurs at a crucial place in the manuscript. Did these goers-before consist of but a trio of men; or did they number three dozen, three score, 300 or 3,000? And were they literally 'cut off' from life by being killed, or merely cut off from their companions by being taken prisoner?

Surely the possibility of there being 3,000 (a significant proportion of York's army) can be discounted, especially if the *English Chronicle* is right about the size of Somerset and Devon's force. Three hundred is more feasible; although as this would presumably have involved a comparable number of opponents it still seems unlikely, given the lack of other contemporary reports, documents pertaining to such a substantial clash in Worksop's town or priory archive, or artefacts attributable to it in the collections of local museums. Camden's *Britannia*, which mentions other 15th century battles including Blore Heath and Towton, refers only to 'Workensop' for 'its great produce of liquorice', while its very own Wars of the Roses battle does not feature in the tourist or promotional literature of the town today. Altogether, this long-standing dearth of interest and information implies not a major encounter but a small scrap between the outriders of two armies, in which no notables were slain on either side. At the other end of the scale, the death or capture of only three individuals seems too trivial for *any* chronicler to record, leaving the more probable figures of 36 to 60 Yorkist goers-before running into a sufficient number of Somerset's men to kill or capture them.

Can anything meaningful be constructed from such minimal evidence? If both armies were making for Worksop for supplies, accommodation and/or because it was a convenient crossing point of the River Ryton, we must infer that the opposing goers-before did not arrive simultaneously. If they had, hostilities would have doubtless ensued – and as their oncoming comrades piled in, it would have turned into a sizeable affray likely to leave more trace in the record and local tradition.

Apparently this did not happen, so a plausible alternative is that Somerset and Devon had arrived at Worksop a good deal earlier than the Yorkist outriders. Most of their men (perhaps led by Devon's contingent, since he is not mentioned in the *Annales*) were already hurrying on; they may have been heading north-east towards Blyth, featured on the 14th century Gough map as a point on the main route between north and south[6] where they could easily pick up a road to Pontefract. Only a straggling remnant of the rearward or baggage train was left by the time York's scouts, or the forerunners of his vanguard, rode up – whereupon a short, sharp fight ensued as the Lancastrians strove to continue their journey, and possibly also to prevent their opponents from riding back with intelligence on their movements. So this entire portion of the Yorkist army might indeed have been destroyed, but it most likely consisted of only a handful of men. Such a scenario fits the existing evidence, and accounts for why there is not more of it: the armies did not fully engage at Worksop because they were some distance apart and on opposite sides of the river. Moreover the weather or light may have been poor, given that the date was approaching midwinter solstice, the shortest day. So even if their respective commanders could see what was going on they may have been too far away to intervene, or unwilling to risk a full-scale attack under such conditions – especially if they were unsure of each others' strength.

Unfortunately, no archaeological evidence has yet come to light to support or refute this conjecture, to pinpoint the site where the conflict took place or give any indication as to its magnitude.[7] One find which at first glance could be taken for a relic of the encounter is preserved in a tiny wall recess at Worksop Priory: a piece of human skull transfixed by a slender needle bodkin arrowhead. The fragment appears to be a right temporal bone pierced to a depth of two to three centimetres, the angle of penetration suggesting the archer was shooting flat rather than lobbing high from long distance. However, although it is consistent with a combat fatality, the skull fragment has no connection with the engagement; it was discovered in 1200 during building works at the Priory, thus pre-dating the battle by 260 years (and according to local tradition, comes from a poacher shot by Robin Hood).

Another suggestion is that the skirmish *did* involve some hundreds of men, and occurred not at Worksop but a few miles to the south at Cuckney[8] (the Latin *'apud Worsop'* may be translated as 'at', 'in', 'beside' or 'near' Worksop). Castle Hill in Cuckney is the site of a 12th century motte-and-bailey, and a Norman church where in 1951, National Coal Board workmen underpinning the foundations uncovered several broad trenches containing at least 200 skeletons, lying east-west (ie Christian burials) and described, albeit without expert verification, as 'young males'. Could they be casualties from the Battle of Worksop? Sadly, the answer again seems to be 'no'; the graves must pre-date the church as they extend beneath its north wall, making them more likely to be associated with the 12th century wars between Stephen and Matilda.[9] Indeed, St Mary's Church may have been built or extended at this time to hallow their remains – and given the early medieval form of the arrowhead discussed above, the skull fragment at Worksop Priory may come from a victim of the same conflict. It is nonetheless frustrating that the Cuckney remains were re-interred without forensic analysis or dating to confirm their age.

To conclude, although the *Annales Rerum Anglicarum* indicates that *something* happened near Worksop around 21st December 1460, the lack of further evidence suggests it was a lesser event than the destruction of the Duke's entire vanguard. More probably, the Yorkists lost between three dozen to 60 troops: scouts, forerunners of the vanguard (possibly riding ahead seeking accommodation or provisions), and/or an advance party making for Sandal Castle. Too little is known of the circumstances or any Lancastrian losses sustained for York to be accused of negligence; the Worksop incident was simply a minor accident of war.

The Myth of York's Rashness

After dealing with whatever consequences they found on reaching Worksop, York and his comrades completed their journey to Wakefield, arriving at Sandal Castle on or soon after 21st December. Christmas must have been passed in a state of considerable tension as the commanders discussed strategies for the impending battle and planned for victory over their enemies. But by the end of the month York was dead, and the manner of his passing has left an enduring 'mystery': why this seasoned warlord made the apparently foolish decision to leave the safety of his castle to engage a force that greatly outnumbered his own.

One explanation developed since the 15th century is that the Duke of York was a bad commander poorly prepared for his northern campaign, with ill-disciplined troops and unreliable intelligence, who recklessly took to the field against the advice of wiser friends. Subscribers to this view quote his unsuccessful attempt to secure the throne in October 1460, the alleged 'destruction' of his vanguard at Worksop, and the catastrophe of Wakefield itself. Countering it may be set the rest of York's career: his exercise of good lordship in the management of his own estates, prudent governance of Normandy, popularity and success as Lieutenant of Ireland, effective rule of England during two protectorates, and his strategic withdrawal at Ludford Bridge when faced with insuperable odds.

Regarding the Duke's conduct at Wakefield, most contemporary and near-contemporary accounts confine themselves to brief reportage of the battle, without castigating what proved to be an ill-fated decision to ride out. The earliest accusation of rashness comes from Francesco Coppini in his letter dated January 9th 1461 to Master Lorenzo de Florencia[10] - although Coppini is in fact denigrating *both* sides, describing the Lancastrians as having won a 'trifling victory' only 'owing to the rash advance of their opponents.'

The First Continuation of the *Crowland Chronicles* also says that 'Richard Duke of York incautiously engaged the northern army at Wakefield... without waiting to bring up the whole of his own forces.'[11] The latter may be the source used and elaborated upon in the 16th century by Polydore Vergil, who says that 'some there were thought it not meet to join battle before his son Edward should come with new forces.'[12] Edward Halle echoes this, saying that the Duke 'determined incontinent to issue out', building the tale up further with his well-known, typically colourful report of York's furious rebuttal of Sir David Halle's prudent counsel, quoted in the **Introduction** and widely repeated.[13] John Stow's *Annales* closely paraphrase Vergil with 'contrary to the mind of his faithful friends [the duke] would needs issue forth to fight with his enemies'[14] – and thus a myth was born.

But does it bear close examination? The extent to which the sources can be trusted is debatable; their details are often inaccurate (for instance, Polydore Vergil believed Wakefield to be 'about 15 miles west of York' instead of some 30 miles south-west, and wrongly placed Queen Margaret on the battlefield); moreover, it was as easy for contemporary commentators to be wise after the event as it is for modern historians. York's army was overwhelmed by a much larger force, which it would not have been had he remained in his castle, ergo he was rash to emerge – and surely some of his advisors would have counselled against it?

Of course, it is highly doubtful that any chroniclers could have known what was said in the Duke's policy discussions at Sandal Castle. Those closest to him - Rutland, Salisbury and sundry others including David Halle - were all either killed in the battle or executed shortly afterwards. Edward Halle's story in particular should be treated with scepticism, although it often forms the basis of modern accounts.[15] Some of his facts are demonstrably incorrect, and his lengthy verbatim speeches must be seen for what they are: dramatised reconstructions, or 'imaginary speeches' as Clement Markham put it.[16] Besides, he had a vested interest in representing David Halle as the voice of reason: Sir David was his grandfather whose advice, if heeded, could have been York's salvation. If there was, as has been suggested, any 'family tradition' to that effect[17] it may have been more along the lines of 'Grandfather Davey was too wise to counsel such madness'. It is also worth mentioning that Johnson's detailed academic biography does not identify David Halle as one of the servants and annuitants with proven connections to the Duke.[18] This at least raises a question mark regarding Sir David's level of involvement with York, and invites the supposition that Edward Halle, for reasons of family pride, exaggerated his role and degree of influence.

As to waiting for reinforcements to arrive, how viable an option was this? Warwick had to remain in London, 'caretaking' Henry VI, while Edward was occupied in the Welsh Marches. It would have taken several days of hard riding to summon either one, then a considerable time to get their forces to Wakefield, putting any subsequent engagement well into January 1461. Meanwhile there was an army to shelter and feed, with the ever-increasing likelihood that Sandal Castle would be besieged and the Yorkists it could not accommodate captured or killed. In contrast, sallying forth under what he reasonably believed to be favourable circumstances must have seemed to the Duke (and his companions) the best, arguably the only sensible action.

Equally, a prolonged siege or war of attrition around the castle would have been just as unattractive to the Lancastrians, with their large force exposed in the winter landscape, vulnerable to attack by Yorkist reinforcements and the attendant risk of being caught in a pincer movement by the Duke's troops. The course events took suggests that they were well aware of this, hence the crux of their battle plan was to draw York out and crush him before March, Warwick or other adherents could come to his aid.

Altogether, there is little to suggest that the Duke of York was viewed as rash by his contemporaries. Coppini flings the accusation to belittle the Lancastrian victory and pop their pride, while the Crowland Chronicler thinks York incautious because he did not wait for reinforcements. Like 'armchair generals' throughout history, the prudent chronicler is entitled to his opinion; but it is *only* an opinion, expressed by someone who did not consider its full implication and did not face the dangerous prospect of spending weeks under siege in the depths of winter. As to 'evidence' that the Duke acted with cavalier disregard to good advice, this comes largely from chroniclers writing decades after the event, one of whom (Halle) can be unreliable and has good reason to be biased. That later writers have believed, repeated and embroidered these accounts with additional assumptions of their own does not elevate them from opinion to fact.

Considered overall, the Duke of York's career does not indicate that he was generally foolish or reckless, although he was plainly capable of misjudgement – evinced by his misapprehension in October 1460 that no-one could possibly prefer the continuing misrule of King Henry's self-interested cronies to his own proven, competent governance. But it is only in retrospect that his actions at Wakefield appear as another misjudgement; at the time, his decision to ride out was perfectly sound, based on his understanding of the situation. York did not lead a mad death-or-glory charge against a force he knew to be much larger, or in ignorance of substantial bodies of troops lying hidden in the landscape. He seized what appeared to be a good military opportunity – and in doing so, was less rash than deliberately deceived by a cunning and plausible enemy.

The Myth of the Foraging Party

Variations on this theme appear frequently: York, seeing from the towers of Sandal Castle that one of his numerous foraging parties was being attacked, charged out pell-mell to the rescue - despite his numbers being sorely depleted by the absence of said foragers. Markham believed that Lord Clifford attacked Yorkist foragers returning from Wakefield, and 'the chivalrous Duke spurned the idea of leaving his foraging party to be destroyed without making an effort at rescue',[19] while Leadman contended that 'the foraging party sent out on Monday 29th ventured too near the enemy... the Yorkists were hotly chased and forced to retire within the walls of Sandal Castle.'[20] This story is stated with the force of proven fact by some historians,[21] and even more sceptical analyses give it credence.[22]

Yet the evidence for the role of foragers in York's defeat is slight and ambiguous. The closest contemporary reference comes in a letter from Antonio de la Torre to Francesco Sforza, Duke of Milan, dated 9th January 1461.[23] It is worth quoting the relevant passage in full for the glaring inaccuracies it contains:

Some of the lords of the queen's party, rendered desperate by the victory of the lords here [ie the Yorkist victory and seizure of Henry VI at Northampton, followed by the Act of Accord] *and especially the Earl of Warwick, assembled a force in the northern parts, eighty miles from London, to come and attack their opponents here who are with the king, and get the king back into their power as they had him before. Accordingly the Duke of York, with two of his sons and Warwick's father, the Earl of Salisbury, went out to meet them. And it came to pass that although they were* three *times stronger* [my emphasis] *yet from lack of discipline, because they allowed a large part of the force to go pillaging and searching for victuals, their adversaries, who are desperate, attacked the duke and his followers. Ultimately they routed them, slaying the duke and his younger son the Earl of Rutland, Warwick's father and many others.*

Compare this with Coppini's letter of the same date (*op cit*):

Tell those lords, and especially the Duke of Somerset, whom we admire for his character and because we believe that he loves the queen and her estate as we do ourselves, that if they do not attend to our advice they will bring desolation upon the whole realm and the estate and wellbeing of his Majesty. They must not be arrogant because of the trifling victory they won, owing to the rash advance of their opponents, [Wakefield] because we have seen and know full well that all the people are incensed and in the worst possible humour against those who do not desire peace. There are two reasons for this: firstly, the countless acts of cruelty related of them, whereas those here [the Yorkist lords] were not cruel, but received into favour those who wished to come; secondly, because they recognise and know that his Majesty and the lords with him and ourself with them are really disposed to an honest and honourable peace, salutary for both parties. Therefore if your influence with them does not suffice, their cause will be in the worst possible case, because the feelings of the people are incredibly incensed against them, and they will see more than two hundred thousand desperate men rise against them, who are constantly assembling, offering to devote their goods and their persons in such an honest and just cause.

Unpicking this fascinating web of information, misinformation, outright mistakes and Yorkist propaganda (the Earl of Warwick was at this time in regular contact with Antonio de la Torre and, like Coppini, corresponding with Pope Pius II) is, sadly, beyond the scope of this work. To consider only those elements pertaining directly to the Battle of Wakefield: it appears that de la Torre believed the Yorkist army to be three times stronger than the Lancastrian; and this numerical superiority notwithstanding, it was defeated because so many undisciplined troops were away pillaging for supplies. This is not supported by logic, (the Lancastrian camp contained a far greater proportion of major magnates than did York's), nor is it borne out by any other contemporary or near-contemporary estimates of the size of the forces:

Annales Rerum Anglicarum:	one version gives 6,000 Yorkists
Benet's Chronicle:	12,000 Yorkists, 20,000 Lancastrians
Gregory's Chronicle:	15,000 Lancastrians
Edward Halle:	<5,000 Yorkists, 18 – 22,000 Lancastrians

Unfortunately we do not know which, if any, of these figures are correct. The best we can say is that the Lancastrian army seems to have significantly outnumbered the Yorkist - perhaps by a factor of three - not *vice versa*. Whatever the truth, it seems highly improbable that the Duke would have allowed a large proportion of his army to be away foraging when he knew battle was imminent, which raises an intriguing possibility. Perhaps the Milanese de la Torre, who was plainly ignorant of the distance between London and Yorkshire and under the misapprehension that the Earl of March was with his father, made another mistake: he confused the behaviour of Queen Margaret's under-paid armies mustered in the north, and incorrectly attributed both their superior size and undisciplined pillaging to the Yorkists. (De la Torre's account also implies that the Lancastrians took advantage of York's reduced numbers to attack 'the duke and his followers', which is also inaccurate; the Lancastrians plainly did not assail Sandal Castle, and could hardly have attacked if the Duke had not elected to emerge).

Certainly, allegations of Yorkist indiscipline or serious depletion of the Duke's army by foraging parties do not feature in other contemporary accounts. A passing reference in *Whethamsted's Register* says that the Yorkist lords 'relaxed in their castles and went foraging for victuals' (something of a contradiction in terms). Foraging is also mentioned in the *Annales Rerum Anglicarum*, though it says only that 'on the twenty-ninth day of the month of December at Wakefield, while the Duke of York's people were wandering about the district in search of victuals, a horrible battle was fought.' And even this contains an error, as most accounts agree that the Battle of Wakefield was fought on Tuesday 30th December.

Nowhere do the contemporary sources explicitly state that York saw or heard report of foragers being attacked, nor that he rode out precipitately to their rescue… yet this is one explanation for his conduct, (and further justification of the 'rash' epithet), that has been seized upon and so relentlessly repeated it is now widely believed. All that the chroniclers *do* say is that before the battle, York had an unspecified number of people out scouring the country for supplies. This is entirely reasonable. Indeed, both the Duke and the Lancastrian commanders would have needed their foragers out; providing food and firing for thousands of men would have presented a massive logistical problem throughout the campaign that culminated so savagely three months later at Towton. However, supplies in general should have been relatively plentiful since the harvests were in, the beasts had been slaughtered, and folk were preparing for Christmas. Provisions should have been easier to obtain at this point than in the truly lean season when stores were depleted prior to new growth in the spring. (The observance of religious fasts, especially Lent, perhaps served a useful secondary function by making a virtue of necessity and accustoming the populace to tight belts and self-denial).

The most logical first port of call for Yorkist troops to garner supplies would have been Wakefield itself. Knowing the enemy lay nine miles to the east at Pontefract, it seems unlikely and unnecessary for them to have foraged far in that direction, as Leadman contends. There were sources of provisions closer to hand in satellite settlements like Sandal Magna, Milnthorpe and Woodthorpe, and just south and west of the castle, a deer-park and the wetland habitat of the River Calder and its tributaries, where game, fish and waterfowl could have been hunted (Faunal remains from the occupation phase 1450 – 1484 at Sandal Castle include cow, sheep, pig, fallow and red deer, rabbit, chicken, goose and other fowl, swan and carp[24] although these unfortunately cannot be pinpointed to December 1460). It is reasonable to surmise that their efforts were aided by local people, since the army's presence would have acted as a magnet for every tradesman, huckster and heggler in the neighbourhood. They could also have foraged safely in the lands of

Sir John Savile, Steward of Wakefield and Constable of Sandal Castle, whose principal seat lay only five miles to the west at Thornhill. Because Sir John is not mentioned by contemporary sources, it is commonly believed – and taken as further evidence of York's ineptitude – that he had not been informed of developments or prepared the castle to receive his lord, and played no part in events up to and including the battle. This may be true up to a point, especially if messengers sent to warn him of the Duke's imminent arrival had been killed or captured at Worksop. Yet it seems inconceivable that such an important officer could have remained ignorant of Lancastrian activities in the area, or that he did not go to York's aid the moment he heard of his presence at Sandal.

Nor is Clement Markham's suggestion credible; surely any foragers heading back to the castle from Wakefield would have remained safely where they were, rather than marching straight into the approaching Lancastrian army whose forerunners may already have taken up position south of the town. It also seems unreasonable that very large numbers of York's troops were foraging – unless they were hunting in the immediate environs of Sandal Castle, whence they could be swiftly recalled. For those roving farther afield, it would have made more practical sense to forage in small squadrons with carts and pack-horses, than in large unwieldy groups. Perhaps we should assume that the Duke's foragers numbered scores, rather than hundreds or thousands, and were assisted by Savile retainers; and that given the Lancastrians' numerical superiority and the simple deception of their battle plan, the presence or absence of these foragers would have made no difference whatsoever to the outcome on the day.

Finally, for this unfeasible tale to be true, it means that the Duke and his entire army charged out to the foragers' rescue - which simply beggars belief, as Haigh observes.[25] By the time several thousand men could have armed and ridden or run down onto Wakefield Green, any beleaguered foraging party would have long since been captured or killed and their supplies secreted behind the Lancastrian lines. Under the circumstances, the likelihood of York regaining either his foragers or their supplies by a frontal attack would have been minimal, a fact which would surely have been apparent to him.

Nonetheless, historians have woven various theories regarding the role of foragers at Wakefield. The line of reasoning seems to be that since foraging is mentioned in several 15th century sources, it must have been a significant factor either by depleting Yorkist numbers, and/or by precipitating the engagement; and as the Lancastrians plainly did not assault the castle itself, this significance must have been that the Duke rode out to his foragers' defence. Extrapolations of this reasoning include:

- The Duke of York was a poor commander who could not control his troops; too many went out foraging, significantly reducing his strength and contributing to his defeat

- The foragers ventured too close to Pontefract, spurring the Lancastrians to action
- The foragers were attacked by, or themselves attacked, the Lancastrian forces
- Their skirmish was witnessed from (or reported to) Sandal Castle, prompting the Duke to mobilise his entire force in response

All of this assumes a great deal from very little: a couple of references to the *existence* of foragers, and to foraging taking place on December 29th, the day before the battle most likely occurred, while de la Torre's more explicit charge is questionable to say the least.

That both armies had foragers out in the field may be taken as fact, given the pressing need to provision large numbers of people mustered around Pontefract and Wakefield. Beyond that, there is no convincing historical evidence to show that Yorkist foragers were attacked, or that rescuing foragers was a motivation for the Duke to leave Sandal Castle; that depletion by foraging parties played any significant part in determining the battle's outcome seems highly unlikely. York was not greatly outnumbered because he had so many foragers absent, as Seward, for instance, believes.[26] He was outnumbered because Queen Margaret had been vigorously mustering support for almost three months prior to the battle, whereas the Duke had only been preparing to ride north since November.

The Myth of Provocation

Desperate to draw York from his stronghold, the Lancastrians sought to goad him into fury with provocative actions: breaking the 'Christmas truce' by presenting themselves on the field, and/or sending heralds with messages casting aspersions on his manhood and courage – according to some 19th century writers and often repeated in modern accounts, although very little support can be found in contemporary sources. There is no explicit reference to the 'truce' alleged to run until the Feast of Epiphany on January 6th; this seems to be extrapolated from a line in *Whethamsted's Register*, saying that the opposing sides passed Christmas awaiting 'the day appointed between them respecting the time of the battle'. More likely, their accord was only the minimum respite necessary for religious observances, to rest the troops after their arduous marches to Yorkshire – and to allow time for anticipated allies to arrive and complete their respective battle plans. Indeed, given the logistical demands of feeding and sheltering their armies, agreeing to abstain from hostilities for the full 'twelve days of Christmas' was almost certainly a luxury neither side could afford – which undermines any suggestion that York rode out to punish his enemies' perfidy, since a prolonged truce was no more in his best interests than in theirs. As Haigh observes, the idea 'has to be viewed at best with caution, and at worst as having no basis in fact'.[27]

Neither is the 'myth of the taunting heralds' any better supported by contemporary reports. It probably derives from the speech put into York's mouth by Edward Halle:

"…would thou that I, for dread of a scolding woman whose only weapons are her tongue and nails, should incarcerate myself and shut my gates? Then all men might of me wonder and all creatures may of me report dishonour, that a woman made me a dastard!"

Quite possibly the Lancastrians *did* engage in this form of psychological warfare and if so, their taunts may not have improved the Duke's mood. Equally he and his men may have simply dismissed it as a transparent ploy – York was an experienced soldier with nothing to prove in terms of valour either to himself or his adherents. Moreover he was clearly prudent enough, and sufficiently indifferent to potential allegations of cowardice, to withdraw from the field in a hopeless situation – as he did at Ludford Bridge in 1459.

So whilst it may be implied by Halle's dramatised account, there is no hard evidence to show that the Duke of York was insulted by Lancastrian heralds. Equally, there is no evidence to prove he was *not*, and this was seized upon by Victorian commentators to explain why York chose to leave his fortified position – perhaps saying more about their romanticised notions of chivalry than about the realities of medieval warfare. Either way, such a tactic would not have been sufficient of itself to lure the Duke forth – especially when a far more convincing and reliable strategy was being prepared by the Lancastrian commanders, as discussed in the next chapter.

The Myth of the Men in the Woods

The crux of many explanations for York's conduct is that he was caught in a cunning trap, the Lancastrians having concealed troops in belts of woodland and/or behind ridges of high ground to disguise their true strength. The relatively small size of their visible forces lulled him into a false sense of superiority, luring him out to give battle; and when his army was fully exposed on Wakefield Green, these hidden troops charged out to surround and overwhelm him.[28] In justification, Markham[29] describes the Sandal landscape as 'partly wooded', although he gives no evidence to support this assertion. Leadman[30] goes a good deal further; in his version, as the main body of Lancastrians advanced, 'so very carefully did the leaders arrange their troops that the greater portion lay in ambush. The castle was completely environed whilst the Duke remained in utter ignorance'; and when battle was joined, 'ambuscades [that] lay behind the castle on both sides issued simultaneously from the woods that had hidden them – light horse led by Lord Rosse [sic] and light foot under Wiltshire', with no source or substantiation offered for these details.

Once again, there is no contemporary support for these statements. The sources are frustratingly laconic on every aspect of the armies' approaches to and disposition on the field, although one factor they have in common is that *none* make any mention of woodlands, concealed armies or complex outflanking manoeuvres.

So the 'men in the woods' story appears to be built upon flimsy foundations: the 16th century accounts by Polydore Vergil and Edward Halle, respectively describing York's force as 'environed of the multitude' and 'environed on every side, like a fish in a net, or a deer in a buck-stall'. Based on the premise that no sane commander would knowingly leave a fortified position to attack a large army with a small one, this has been taken to mean that Lancastrian troops had lain hidden in nearby woods, waiting to ambush and surround York. Thus either the Duke was madly reckless, and/or failed to realise how big the opposing army was, ergo a substantial portion of it must have been concealed.

So commentators state and re-state that York rode out to fight the army he could see, having no inkling of the true size of the host he was facing; but struggle to explain exactly *how* the Lancastrians managed to manoeuvre and conceal large numbers of men within a mile of Sandal Castle, its neighbouring settlements and the Yorkist army mustered in its environs. None have done so convincingly. After all, if the Duke thought he could successfully engage the forces in plain view with the 5,000 - 6,000 troops he most probably had, it means the Lancastrians somehow smuggled a sizeable force past his look-outs, and secreted them on the land for some time without anyone noticing. Moreover, they accomplished this literally in the 'back garden' of one of his residences, a castle commanding excellent views over a landscape with which the Duke and his staff would presumably have been very familiar.

It is an idea that stretches credulity to the limits, especially in the presence of conclusive proof that areas of ground between Sandal Castle and Wakefield, and in their general environs, were *not* forested but under cultivation (see Fig. 2 and Plate 7). Fields of ridge-and-furrow still remain adjacent to the traditional site of York's fall, less than half a mile north of the castle (a remnant of Wakefield Green, now Castle Grove Park); in the grounds of Sandal Endowed School at Sandal Magna, and farther south-east beside the Walton road; a mile due south, along the banks of Owler Beck at Kettlethorpe; and beyond the River Calder, west of Fall Ings, in what is now Thornes and Clarence Park. Other fragments are illustrated on 19th century Ordnance Survey maps adjacent to the river and the road leading to Wakefield Bridge in Fall Ings; and John Leland's *Itinerary* of 1534 includes the remark, 'there was a sore Batell faught in the south Feeldes by this Bridge.'[31]

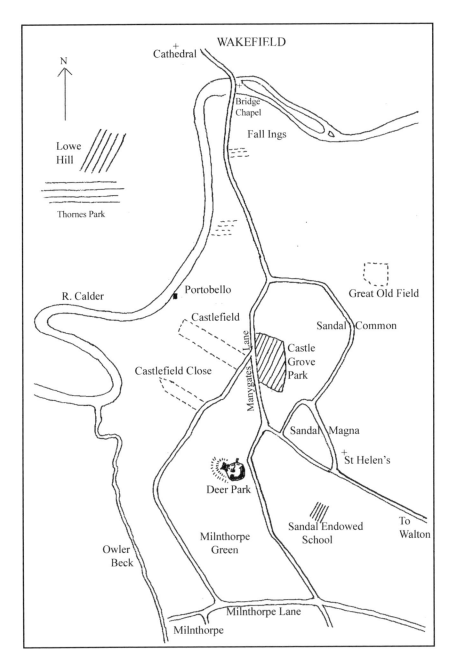

Figure 2: Map of Wakefield showing features referred to in the text. Solid lines are extant ridge-and-furrow; broken lines are fields and ridge-and-furrow lost since the 1800 Enclosure map and 19th century Ordnance Survey map. The black square at Portobello marks the site of Portobello House (now demolished).

The 1800 Enclosure map indicates that the whole area around the castle was enclosed by that date, with large fields to the south and west bounded by Milnthorpe Lane. 'Castle Field' and 'Castle Field Close' are both identified to the north/north-west of the castle; there is also a 'Great Old Field' north of Sandal Magna beside the Doncaster turnpike. In the accompanying ledger of awards, Castle Field, Great Old Field and other allotments in the vicinity of Sandal Castle, for example Cock and Bottle Lane, (now Manygates Lane), Milnthorpe Green and Sandal Common are most commonly described as abutting 'old inclosures' – in other words, fields were present long before 1800 – and there is no mention of woodland in any of these areas. All this suggests that rather than forest, there was a large stretch of arable land and open common between the castle and town – corresponding with the 'plain field' alluded to in Stow's *Annales* as the site of the battle. The existence of farmland is further confirmed by pollen analysis and plant remains from excavations at Sandal Castle, indicative of cereal cultivation in its environs.

However, plant remains also confirm the proximity of mixed oak, birch and willow woodland, consistent with historical references and maps evincing the presence of a paled deer-park near the castle. The existence of an 'adjoining' well-paled park of about 40 acres and containing about 30 fallow deer is mentioned in a survey of 1545 – 6; in a survey of 1564, Sandal's park is described as being 32 acres with about 20 deer, but instead of 'adjoining' it, 'the Castell standeth therein'. This later survey also mentions the 'old park' of Wakefield, containing 30 deer, and the 'new park' which must have been substantially larger, given that it had a deer population of 300. And according to the survey of 1565 – 6, there was 'sufficient of all kind of timber of Her Majesty's possessings within the park at Sandal and in the outwoods of Wakefield, being within two miles of the said Castle' to carry out structural repairs there.[32]

So woodland *was* present in the vicinity – but whereabouts? Unfortunately, there are no detailed 15th century maps of the area to answer this question, and even the earliest date to 150 years after our period of interest. These are John Speed's Yorkshire maps of c. 1610, showing that both the 'old' and 'new' parks were well away from the battlefield, to the north-east and north-west of Wakefield respectively and separated by the village of Wrenthorpe (see Plate 8). Speed labels the new park, bisected by a tributary of the River Calder (probably Balne Beck), and also shows the paled park at Sandal, although it is unclear whether he intends to show the park encircling the castle or lying to the west between it and Owler Beck. Henry Overton's map of 1711 also depicts Wakefield's old and new parks with their fences intact, but by this date the paled park at Sandal has disappeared; all his map shows is a scatter of trees to the south-west of the castle.

Plate 7: Ridge-and-furrow in Castle Grove Park, near the site of York's fall.

Plate 8: Detail of Speed's 1610 map showing the deer-parks at Wakefield and Sandal. Photo by Sally Mills; reproduced by kind permission of West Yorkshire Archive Service, Wakefield, ref. C559/76.

Given the extant ridge-and-furrow a short distance to the north, it seems unlikely that Sandal Castle was fully encircled by a paled park in the 15th century. More probably, the deer-park adjoined it to the south as described in the 1545 – 6 survey and further suggested by a drawing dated 1562, generated by a draughtsman standing north of the castle with the keep on his right and the state buildings of the bailey on his left (see Plate 9). Plainly, his view of the north elevation was not obstructed by trees; however, a century after our period of interest, there are trees to the east and west apparently growing in the outer moat. A tree to the south can also be glimpsed between the tiled kitchen roof and the ornate chimney and turret of the state lodgings. This is consistent with the site's documented deterioration, and vegetation having encroached from a south-lying park as far as the outer defences (a situation unlikely to have been tolerated in York's day, but which may account for later confusion as to whether Sandal Castle stood within or adjacent to its deer-park).

Plate 9: Sandal Castle, 1562, drawn from 'Duchy of Lancaster Maps and Plans 1562 – 4', The National Archives, MPC 1/97. On the left are the great hall, great chamber, chapel and lodgings; in the foreground, timber-framed lodgings with ornate chimneys probably erected after 1475; and left of centre is the barbican. The gatehouse is in the centre foreground, with an arcaded passage leading to the keep; behind it are a large bake-house chimney and kitchen roof with gabled smoke louvre. In the right foreground are the Constable's lodgings. The square tower on the far right was added c. 1484 by Richard III. The extent to which trees have encroached from the south can clearly be seen.

Sadly lacking from this discussion is *conclusive* evidence regarding the precise extent, nature and position of Sandal Park and any other areas of woodland in the immediate vicinity of the castle. The tree-line positions represented on Philip Haigh's battlefield maps are, as the author concedes, purely conjectural,[33] although it is reasonable to guess that the banks of the Calder were bordered with trees including willow. However, if the fields between Sandal and Wakefield were in fact bounded by woods on one or both sides, we do not know their density or extent – only that in December there would have been no leaf cover, making it even less likely that substantial bodies of men (and horses?) could have moved through or remained hidden among them. Moreover, to enter any putative woodland along the Calder bank, the Lancastrians would either have had to cross the fields in front of Sandal Castle, break through the fenced park behind it, or circle further south past Milnthorpe – all without detection. This is an unlikely scenario, especially if the park was under guard or even under occupation by Yorkist soldiers, as it might well have been. The influx of horses, from noble mounts to pack animals, would surely have filled all the equine accommodation in the Sandal area; and the deer-park, with a defensible perimeter and the shelter afforded by its trees, would make it an obvious place to keep animals that could not be stabled elsewhere.

Plate 10: Environs of Sandal Castle showing the conjectured positions of the deer-park and Yorkist camp. Photo by Roger Keech, © RK Stills 2007.

Accounts of the battle suggesting that York's army was caught in an ambush by hidden troops therefore rest upon a very shaky premise: the existence of convenient belts of woodland either side of Wakefield Green. This is not supported by existing evidence, (Tudor surveys, 17th, 18th and 19th century maps, ridge-and-furrow traces), which shows instead that the battlefield site was a system of open fields, with the documented woodland lying north of the town (too far away to have featured in any such battle plan), and Sandal Park occupying 30 – 40 acres most probably to the south/south-west of the castle. The latter was a paled deer-park overlooked by Sandal Castle, an area of managed land (not necessarily thickly wooded) very familiar to the Duke's staff, and possibly the source of some of the charcoal remains found during excavation – altogether, an unlikely place for the Lancastrians to penetrate and hide in. So, given the complete lack of contemporary references and the inability of modern commentators to explain how the manoeuvre was achieved, the obvious conclusion is that it simply did not happen; there were no such woods; there was no such ambush.

However, one plausible recent theory regarding 'hidden' Lancastrian troops does not rely on large numbers of men lurking among non-existent trees. In his discussion of the local topography, Richard Knowles describes how the main approach from Pontefract to Wakefield is partially screened from Sandal Castle by a ridge of high ground between the villages of Crofton and Walton.[34] Following on from this, David Cooke offers the pragmatic suggestion that the army York thought he could successfully engage was only the Lancastrian vanguard, while the mainward and rearward followed some distance behind, obscured from view by the lie of the land; it was the subsequent arrival of these troops that swung the battle decisively against the Yorkists[35] and could account for the descriptions of their 'environing.'

This is an elegantly simple solution to the conundrum of Wakefield, albeit one that dismisses the role of Lord Neville (discussed in the next chapter) and which does not feature in any contemporary chronicles. Furthermore, it hinges on two factors as uncertain to present-day commentators as they would have been to the Lancastrians: the quality of Yorkist intelligence and whether the approach of many more troops really *could* have been successfully screened by the landscape until the Duke was irrevocably committed to action.

Cooke's theory also raises some interesting questions. Was the staggered arrival he proposes a deliberate ploy or a lucky accident (as with the timely arrival of the Duke of Norfolk's troops at Towton)? If deliberate, it was a finely-calculated risk: the exposure of a force small enough to entice York out in the expectation of victory, but large enough to hold their own until the reinforcements arrived. It could not have been certainly known that the Duke *would* promptly respond to this provocation - or that he would not be forewarned of the main army's approach and withdraw to his castle, possibly after inflicting heavy casualties on the vanguard. Alternatively, did York know or surmise that this was only the advance guard, and ride out on a calculated risk of his own to try and deplete the enemy forces? In either case, it would have been a perilous venture wherein everything hung on the timing. Another possibility is that any staggered arrival was merely the by-product of deploying a large army, in which case York's premature emergence was the lucky accident, from a Lancastrian perspective. Other points to bear in mind are that:

- We have no accurate picture of the 15th century landscape around Sandal Castle: the nature and precise route of main roads and minor track-ways, the level of tree cover, the extent of settlements etc
- We do not know the exact route taken by the Lancastrian army: whether they adhered to main routes or deviated across country to take advantage of landscape screening
- We do not know whether the Yorkists had scouts watching the approaches
- We do not know how well the Lancastrians knew the country or the extent to which their approach would be screened – had they been scouting the routes in preparation for this battle plan?

Altogether, the theory put forward by Knowles and Cooke is far more persuasive than the 'men in the woods' scenario. Nonetheless, it raises as many questions as it answers, and by itself seems insufficient to explain the events of 30th December. (Some suggestions on how this and other theories might be tested appear in **Chapter 6**).

Myths of the Battle

Very few details survive with respect to the actual conduct of the Battle of Wakefield. Collating the contemporary sources gives the following bald summary:

On 30th December 1460, a horrible battle was fought between supporters of Richard, Duke of York and Queen Margaret, on the plain ground between Sandal Castle and Wakefield. The Duke's army included his son Edmund, Earl of Rutland, the Earl of Salisbury, and Salisbury's son Sir Thomas Neville; the Queen's army included the Duke of Somerset, the Earls of Northumberland, Devon and Wiltshire and the Lords Clifford, Dacre, Neville, Roos and Latimer. At first the fight was fiercely contested but the smaller Yorkist army was soon surrounded and routed. The Duke of York was killed together with around 2,000 of his supporters; the Earl of Rutland was killed by Lord Clifford near Wakefield; the Earl of Salisbury was captured and beheaded the following day at Pontefract.

The majority of 15th century reports say little more than this apart from naming some other combatants slain, while 16th century writers go slightly further. Edward Halle is the only chronicler to offer any clue regarding troop deployments, placing the Duke of Somerset in the centre battle, with Lord Clifford and the Earl of Wiltshire in the 'stoles'. The word 'stole' is interpreted by some historians to mean 'ambush', but if we discount the 'men in the woods' theory, it is more likely to mean the stalls, or left and right battles of the classic 15th century formation.

As to the course of action, Polydore Vergil states that: 'At the beginning the fight was mightily maintained mutually, while that a great part of them who were in the front battle being killed, the Duke of York's small number was environed of the multitude.' This may be the source drawn on (and embroidered) by Edward Halle with his famous line, 'environed on every side like a fish in a net or a deer in a buck-stall', and echoed more simply by John Stow with 'when he was in the plain ground between his castle and the town of Wakefield, he was environed on every side.'

Such are the minimal accounts inflated by Victorian writers into highly colourful, dramatised reconstructions which still receive credence today, despite being unsupported by evidence and in some respects demonstrably wrong. Clement Markham, for instance, has the Yorkist army emerging from a south-facing gateway and circling Sandal Castle to face the enemy, a mistake recently repeated[36] - even though logic dictates and excavation has proved that the castle's only gateway faces north, overlooking the main road between Sandal and Wakefield. Presumably elaborating on Halle, Markham also claims that Lord Clifford led the van, or right battle, with his flank on the River Calder; the Dukes of Somerset and Exeter, and the Earls of Devon and Northumberland were in the centre; and the Earl of Wiltshire led the rear, or left battle, with Andrew Trollope as their 'principal adviser and chief of staff', a detail which can only have come from Jean de Waurin. However, Markham gives no source or substantiation for his troop dispositions, inviting the conclusion that he simply made it up.

Other Victorian fabrications come from Stansfield, replete with purple prose, unsupported assumptions and unknown, unknowable details – York unhorsed, wounded and beaten to his knees, his gallant supporters swept away, until 'a hundred blows rained down on the Duke's armour, and he at last fell, still grasping his sword in his iron hand.'[37] While such accounts are undeniably atmospheric they are the stuff of romantic novels, not historical fact, and do not make much valid contribution to an understanding of events on the day.

Thankfully, most modern commentators are more restrained in their treatment, if no better supported in their reconstruction of events. Alison Weir has the right and left flanks, commanded by Wiltshire and Roos, hiding in the mythical woods. Lawrence Butler, adhering to the 'ambush environing' theory, names Lord Clifford as leading an attack from the south of Sandal Castle up Milnthorpe Lane, a manoeuvre contradicted by contemporary evidence placing Clifford to the north of the battlefield (see **Chapter 4**). Keith Dockray contends that York, 'throwing caution to the winds… chose to lead his men in a wild rush down the castle hill', while Haigh agrees that 'the usual preambles were ignored at this battle and the two sides plunged straight in to the deadly melee.'[38]

But the fact is that we do not (and probably never will) know the fine detail of the Battle of Wakefield. We can only estimate the size of the armies and the casualty figures from widely varying contemporary reports – reports which tell nothing of routes to the battlefield, weather conditions, troop disposition, battlefield tactics and the relative proportion of cavalry, archers and foot-soldiers on the opposing sides. Neither do they tell us whether either side possessed artillery, whether the encounter opened with the usual archery exchanges, or indeed any of the other information required to develop an accurate picture of what took place. Hence widely-read accounts of the battle often contain fanciful reconstructions which are inconsistent with the scanty evidence that does exist regarding the nature of the battlefield and the position of named combatants.

The Myth of the Ant-hill Throne

Richard of York was not killed outright in the fighting, but captured and subjected to a grotesque humiliation before being executed on the field. The origin of this tale seems to be *Whethamsted's Register*, which says that the Lancastrians 'stood him on a little anthill and placed on his head, as if a crown, a vile garland made of reeds'[39] while Halle later has York's head crowned with paper, albeit after his posthumous decapitation by Lord Clifford. It was an image too good for Shakespeare to resist:

Q. Margaret: Brave warriors, Clifford and Northumberland,
             Come, make him stand upon this molehill here…

             A crown for York! And lords, bow low to him:
             Hold you his hands, whilst I do set it on
                            [Putting a paper crown on his head

             Ay, marry, sir, now he looks like a king...
             Off with his head, and set it on York gates:
             So York may overlook the town of York
                            [Flourish. Exeunt.

                            King Henry the Sixth, Part 3, Scene 4

70

This is marvellous stuff, which like all Shakespeare's historical plays has left an indelible imprint on the national consciousness; and like them all, it is highly-coloured drama, not historical fact - it places all four of York's sons, including the children George and Richard, at Wakefield with their father, while Queen Margaret, along with Lord Clifford, is responsible for stabbing the Duke to death. Nonetheless, variations of the story occasionally surface in modern accounts: Weir has the Duke's corpse propped against an ant-hill crowned with reeds; Seward reports that Tudor chroniclers describe him as 'crowned with bulrushes... and made to stand on a molehill before being beheaded.'[40] It also appears in Johnson's biography with the note that 'James Luttrell, a Devon squire, was later charged with the crime'[41] implying that Luttrell was responsible for this act. However, the relevant reference in the Calendar of Patent Rolls says only that:

James who died after 29th December, 39 Henry VI, and before 4th March, 1 Edward IV [perhaps of wounds sustained at the Battle of Wakefield?]... for his murder of the king's father Richard, late Duke of York, be attainted of high treason and forfeit to the king all his possessions...' [42]

Luttrell's attainder was ordained at Westminster on 4th November 1461 – seven months after King Edward's Act of Attainder named numerous other individuals including the Duke of Somerset as having, 'with grete despite and cruell violence, horrible and unmanly tyranny murdered the seid right noble Prynce Duke of York.' In effect, James Luttrell was only one of the Lancastrians identified and punished by Edward IV for having played a significant part in his father's death, which the Yorkists understandably viewed as murder. It does not prove they literally killed the Duke with their own hands, nor that Luttrell executed York or placed any sort of mock crown on his head.

Altogether, the 'anthill throne' anecdote smacks of the medieval version of the 'urban myth', a nice blend of fact and fiction circulated without too much consideration of its plausibility. John Whethamsted plainly deplored the conduct of the Lancastrian army as it pillaged its way towards the second Battle of St Albans; possibly this atrocity story is his counter-strike, a malicious invention calculated to show the Lancastrians in the worst possible light. But could there have been an ant-hill, as the abbot alleges? The yellow field ant builds small hills in limestone/chalk grassland, but the land between Sandal Castle and Wakefield is not chalky; moreover, an ant-hill large enough to stand on, let alone prop a corpse against, would have sorely inconvenienced any farmer and is unlikely to have survived the harvest and subsequent ploughing in the autumn of 1460. Wood ants build much larger nesting mounds, typically in coniferous forests where they can reinforce the hills with pine-needles; but the battle was fought on farmland, not in a pinewood. The mole is a more likely candidate for the building of hills on Wakefield Green in December, although for an exercise in humiliation, the eminence it generates is paltry – and as easily squashed as this story. As to the 'crowning': conceivably, reeds or bulrushes could have been obtained on the battlefield, from field ditches or the banks of the Calder. Less plausible is the idea that someone took to the field conveniently armed with a sheet of paper (unless there was a secretary attached to the Lancastrian army).

Thus it seems highly improbable that the Duke of York was humiliated in such a way prior to execution, let alone that it was done for Margaret of Anjou's edification. Contemporary sources state that the Duke was killed in the fighting rather than executed afterwards, while (contrary to Polydore Vergil's account) the Queen is generally believed to have been far from Wakefield at the time of the battle, probably in Scotland seeking further support from Mary of Guelders.[43]

However, the story of York's *head* being posthumously dishonoured is more widely attested, and far more credible as a Lancastrian device for mocking his pretensions to the throne. The Duke and his son were not the only casualties to be decapitated after death; various sources name Sir Thomas Neville, Edward Bourchier, Sir Thomas Harrington, Thomas Parre, James Pickering, John Harrow and Captain Hanson as having been treated in similar fashion. The heads, along with the Earl of Salisbury's, were sent to be displayed on the gates and 'divers parts' of York. Vergil says that they were put upon stakes and carried to the city 'for a spectacle to the people and a terror to the rest of the adversaries', and it is easy to envisage the Duke's head being distinguished by a paper crown for this grisly parade.

The Myth of Hapless Young Rutland

Edward Halle gives a pathetic account of this fair and maiden-like 12-year-old, under the guardianship of his schoolteacher and chaplain Sir Robert Aspall, mercilessly stabbed through the heart by 'Bloodsupper' Clifford in revenge for his father's death at St Albans. The anecdote features in Shakespeare's *King Henry VI* and was much beloved by Victorian writers and artists, frequently immortalised in romantic images of a pretty long-haired child in doublet and hose, begging at the feet of a steely-eyed knight.[44]

But Halle's heavily sensationalised story is demonstrably wrong in one important respect (which has not prevented later historians from dwelling *ad nauseam* upon Rutland's youth). The Earl was 17 and six months, fully adult by 15th century standards; little more than a year younger than his avenger the Earl of March, who ended this shattering campaign as King Edward IV, or his brother Richard, the future Duke of Gloucester, would be when he successfully commanded at Barnet and Tewkesbury in 1471. Described by Gregory as 'one of the best-disposed lords in the land', Rutland was no mere boy but an adult peer of the realm, raised and educated alongside his elder brother and trained from early youth to bear arms. Nonetheless, his role at Wakefield is generally reduced to that of a victim, and it has been suggested that, 'it is not known whether the Earl was involved in the actual battle, or viewed it from some vantage point'[45] - which seems highly unlikely. If the Duke of York had wished his son merely to watch, what better (and safer) vantage point could there have been than Sandal Castle itself? But the well-attested site of his death indicates that Rutland *was* actively involved; indeed, as one of the highest-ranking peers in the Yorkist army he may even have commanded one of the battles, supported by Aspall, who was more probably his tutor-at-arms than his schoolmaster. Then as it became clear that the day was lost and he was unable to reach or aid his father, the Earl's only recourse was to make for the town, but he was slain before he could reach safety.

That Lord Clifford was his executioner is entirely credible; it is also mentioned in the *Annales Rerum Anglicarum* and for once, Edward Halle offers some substantiation for the cruel speech he attributes to Clifford – that he 'bade his chaplain bear the earl's mother and brother word of what he had done, and said.' As to the means of execution, Halle says Rutland was struck to the heart with Clifford's dagger; Michael Miller suggests, picturesquely but quite without foundation, that he was transfixed through the neck so that the point of the dagger emerged at the back.[46]

To look a little closer at reality: Rutland or Aspall may, as Halle claims, have pleaded with Clifford for mercy on the grounds that he was 'a prince's son and may do you good hereafter' – or more prosaically, that he could be ransomed by the Yorkists for a fat sum. If so, Lord Clifford, gripped by the hatred of blood-feud, was not disposed to grant it.

Could Rutland have been struck to the heart? Clearly, a nobleman of the Earl's status would have taken to the field fully armoured (irrespective of whether or not he was an active combatant), while Lord Clifford could well have been armed with a rondel dagger. The rondel was a characteristic 15th century weapon for close-quarter despatch: a long, vicious blade with triangular section, designed to be driven like a hammer through chinks in the armour or to deliver the *coup-de-grace* to a fallen foe.[47] Such a dagger could easily have pierced Rutland's heart if he was stabbed through his unprotected armpit. Alternatively (and perhaps more believably in the circumstances) he was forced to his knees with his helmet removed, and Clifford's rondel punched down through the hollow at the base of his neck, behind the collar-bone into his heart, killing him instantly.

But assuming Rutland died as the chroniclers relate, this was not an adult's murder of a helpless child – it was the execution of an equivalently armed and armoured enemy on the battlefield, by an angry lord deprived of his father thanks to the Yorkists.

This analysis attempts to show that many accepted accounts of the Battle of Wakefield derive from sources which, on closer examination, prove to be questionable and open to alternative interpretation. Sadly we do not possess a range of reliable, eye-witness reports to draw upon; of the documentary evidence that *has* survived, we cannot be certain of its accuracy or the degree to which it is distorted by contemporary rumour, propaganda, misunderstanding or the writers' own personal bias. Therefore beyond these scanty fragments all we have is conjecture, theory and speculation regarding the course of the battle – my own contribution to which appears in the following chapter.

Notes

1. Boardman, *op cit*, p.27.
2. Haigh, *op cit*, p.18.
3. Paul Hindle, *Medieval Roads and Tracks*, Shire Archaeology Number 26, Shire Publications Ltd., 1998, particularly Chapters 1 and 2. The itinerary of Richard III shows him travelling through Salisbury, Dorchester, Exeter, Winchester and Farnham to London in November 1483, and from Westminster to Canterbury, Sandwich and back again in January 1484 – see Rhoda Edwards, *The Itinerary of King Richard III 1483 – 1485*, Allan Sutton Publishing Ltd for the Richard III Society, 1983.
4. Haigh, *op cit*, p.18; his source is *Annales Rerum Anglicarum*, Vol. II pp. 484-5, translated from the Chronicles of the White Rose, LXXXIII, ed. J.C. Giles, 1843.
5. This version of the Latin text appears in Stevenson, *op cit*, p.775; the translation was provided by Lesley Boatwright of the Richard III Society. Interestingly, there are some differences between Stevenson's rendering and an original manuscript copy of the *Annales* held by the College of Arms, f. 170 (recto) of MS. Arundel 48, which gives the date of the adjournment of parliament as *29°. die mensis Decembris* and *militibus* (soldiers) instead of *armatis*.
6. Hindle, *op cit*, Chapter 4 and illustration p. 30.
7. One potential relic of the encounter is a nine-inch medieval spearhead found by the then Ministry of Works in 1957, in an unspecified location near the town; Mark Taylor, 28/4/2009, personal communication. Sadly, I have been unable to find any further information on this artefact, or to establish whether it is of 15th century date.
8. I am indebted to Richard Moore, author of *Off on the Outlaw Trail Again: in North Notts, Derbyshire and Yorkshire*, for this information.
9. M.W. Barley, 'Cuckney Church and Castle', in *Transactions of the Thoroton Society*, No. 775, 1951, pp. 26 – 29; also Nottinghamshire Sites & Monuments Record (SMR), M8707.

10. *Calendar of State Papers and Manuscripts existing in the Archives and Collections of Milan*, (CSPM), A. B. Hinds (ed.), London, 1913; on-line version, British History Online, www.british-history.ac.uk, document 52.

11. *Ingulph's Chronicle of the Abbey of Croyland*, H.T. Riley (ed.), London, 1854, p. 421.

12. Vergil, *op cit*, pp. 108 – 9.

13. Halle, *op cit*, folio xcix.

14. John Stow, *Annales, or a Generall Chronicle of England*, 1615, pp. 683 – 5.

15. For example Alison Weir's account is largely derived from Halle – see *Lancaster & York, The Wars of the Roses*, Jonathan Cape, 1995, pp. 254 – 57.

16. Clement Markham, 'The Battle of Wakefield', *Yorkshire Archaeological Journal*, Vol. 9, 1886, p. 118.

17. Keith Dockray says, 'his ancestor Sir David Hall lost his life at Wakefield and he may have been able to draw on family material relating to the matter (as well as oral tradition)' in 'The Battle of Wakefield and the Wars of the Roses', off-print from *The Ricardian*, Vol. IX, No. 117, June 1992, p. 5.

18. See Appendix III in Johnson, *op cit*, pp. 228 – 241.

19. Markham, *op cit*, p. 113. His view is echoed on the West Yorkshire Archaeology Advisory Service website www.archaeology.wyjs.org.uk: 'On 30th December the Duke of York sent a foraging party from Sandal Castle to find food in Wakefield… A unit of Lancastrians under the command of Lord Clifford came upon the foraging party at Portobello and cut them off from their base. The Duke of York, perhaps mistaking the size of the Lancastrian force, led his men out of the castle to attempt a rescue'.

20. Alex D. H. Leadman, 'The Battle of Wakefield', *Yorkshire Archaeological Journal*, Vol. 11, 1891, p. 354.

21. For example see Lawrence Butler, *Sandal Castle, Wakefield: The History and Archaeology of a Medieval Castle*, Wakefield Historical Publications, 1991, p. 51; Gillingham, *op cit*, p. 122; Michael K. Jones, *Psychology of a Battle: Bosworth 1485*, Tempus Publishing Ltd. 2002, pp. 48 – 49.

22. Philip Haigh discusses the 'foraging party' theory in some depth - *op cit*, Chapter 5.

23. CSPM, *op cit*, document 54.

24. N.J.L. Griffith et al in Chapter 5, 'The Environment', *Sandal Castle Excavations 1964 – 1973*, Philip Mayes and Lawrence Butler, Wakefield Historical Publications, 1983, pp. 341 – 348.

25. Haigh, *op cit*, p. 65.

26. 'Since most of their troops were away foraging, York and Salisbury were heavily outnumbered', says Desmond Seward in *The Wars of the Roses*

and the Lives of Five Men and Women in the Fifteenth Century, Constable and Company Ltd., 1995, p. 62. He continues, 'Sandal was impregnable; had they stayed inside, they could easily have held out until reinforcements reached it' – another highly questionable statement.

27. Haigh, *op cit*, p.20 and notes 19 – 20, p. 164. The Christmas truce theory has recently been re-stated by Pauline Harrison Pogmore, 'Wakefield to Towton (Part 1), *Blanc Sanglier*, Vol. 44, No. 1, December 2009, p. 18, and Trevor Royle, *The Road to Bosworth Field*, Little, Brown, 2009, p.262. The myth of the taunting heralds is cited by historians including Weir, *op cit*, p. 255, and Boardman, *op cit*, p. 26.

28. For example Boardman, *op cit*, p. 29; Miller, *op cit*, Chapter 52 p. 4; Weir, *op cit*, p. 255.

29. Markham, *op cit*, p. 111.

30. Leadman, *op cit*, p. 354.

31. John Leland, 'Itinerary', Yorkshire extracts, *Yorkshire Archaeological Journal*, Vol. 10, 1889, p. 242.

32. The 16th century surveys are given as appendices to Chapter 1 of Mayes and Butler, *op cit*, pp. 19 – 23.

33. Haigh, *op cit*, p.124.

34. Richard Knowles, 'The Battle of Wakefield: the Topography', off-print from *The Ricardian*, Vol. IX, No. 117, June 1992, 22 – 27.

35. David Cooke, *Battlefield Yorkshire, From the Romans to the English Civil Wars*, Pen & Sword Books Ltd., 2006, p.108.

36. Markham, *op cit*, p. 113; Miller, *op cit*, p.4.

37. A. Stansfield, *Sandal Castle and the Battle of Wakefield*, 1891, pp. 40 – 41.

38. Weir, *op cit*, p. 255; Butler, *op cit*, p. 51; Dockray, *op cit*, p. 10; Haigh, *op cit*, p. 50.

39. From *Whethamsted's Register*, quoted in Dockray, *op cit.*, 2000, pp. 99 – 100.

40. Weir, *op cit*, p. 257; Seward, *op cit*, p. 62.

41. Johnson, *op cit*, p. 223.

42. Calendar of Patent Rolls 1467 – 76, p. 522.

43. Maurer, *op cit*, p. 191.

44. For examples of this artwork see Boardman, *op cit*, p. 31 and Haigh, *op cit*, p. 47.

45. Haigh, *op cit*, p. 54.

46. Miller, *op cit*, p. 5.

47. Graeme Rimer, 'Weapons', in *Blood Red Roses: The Archaeology of a Mass Grave from the Battle of Towton AD 1461*, Veronica Fiorato et al (eds.), Oxbow Books, 2007, pp. 122 – 123.

CHAPTER 4: THE *REAL* BATTLE OF WAKEFIELD?

Date of the Battle

Contemporary sources agree that the Battle of Wakefield occurred in late December, although they contain discrepancies regarding the exact date:

Annales Rerum Anglicarum:	29th December
Benet's Chronicle:	30th December
Chronicles of London:	30th December
Fabyan's Chronicle:	30th December
Great Chronicle of London:	30th December
Gregory's Chronicle:	30th December
English Chronicle:	'last day' (ie 31st) December
Short English Chronicle:	New Year's Eve[1]

The present account adheres to the majority view that the battle was fought on the 30th – a date supported by Edward IV's Act of Attainder, stating that his father was killed on 'Tywesday XXX day Decembr.'[2]

The Size of the Armies

While the date of the battle can be pinned down with reasonable confidence, the number of troops is much more difficult to establish. As previously discussed, where the chronicles specify a number (and many do not), there are wide variations ranging from less than 5,000 to 12,000 Yorkists, and 15,000 to 22,000 Lancastrians. Reports of the battle (and indeed its outcome) do suggest that the Lancastrian army was significantly bigger than York's. Beyond that we can only guess which chronicler was the best-informed, although a further clue may lie in the reported casualty figures:

Whethamsted's Register:	700 Yorkists
Benet's Chronicle:	c. 1,000 Yorkists
Annales Rerum Anglicarum:	2,000 Yorkists
English Chronicle:	2,200 Yorkists
Gregory's Chronicle:	2,500 Yorkists, 200 Lancastrians
Edward Halle:	2,800 Yorkists

If these figures represent the Yorkists being wiped out to the last, it follows that the Duke had between 700 (Whethamsted) to 2,800 (Halle) men on the field. But the chroniclers do not mention such complete annihilation; there are references to prisoners being taken to Pontefract, and we know that some Yorkists did survive to fight another day (see **Chapter 5**). So if instead the figures represent a 50% death toll, as may have been sustained in such a disastrous rout, York fielded 1,400 – 5,600 troops; or if we base the calculation on losses of one-third, it gives him 2,100 – 8,400.

This account assumes that the Yorkist army contained approximately 5,000 men, and that their opponents had at least twice, if not three times, that number. If this is anywhere near the truth it makes the Battle of Wakefield among the largest encounters of the Wars of the Roses - and many of the participants went on to fight at Towton, which is frequently quoted as being 'the biggest and bloodiest battle ever to take place on English soil'. It is sometimes assumed that the combatant figures for either or both battles were wildly over-estimated, or exaggerated for propaganda purposes. However, it has recently been suggested that the armies involved were unusually large, and for a plausible reason: this campaign took place in winter, the slackest time of year agriculturally speaking, when men could be more readily spared from the land to go to war[3] (and perhaps were further attracted by the prospects of plunder and the ability to settle long-standing personal grievances). The theory is persuasive - perhaps we *can* safely believe that 15,000 - 20,000 men faced one another across Wakefield Green on 30th December 1460.

The Battlefield

Regarding the battlefield's location, the surviving evidence – documentary, archaeological, topographic and structural – all points to the area bounded by Sandal Castle to the south, the River Calder to the west, and the town of Wakefield with its chantry chapel on the medieval bridge to the north.

Sandal Castle was presumably where York, Rutland, Salisbury and his sons, other favoured supporters and their retinues were billeted in safety and such comfort as the castle could afford. Sandal Castle, a prominent site overlooking a crossing point of the River Calder and once the administrative centre of an extensive manor, was both a stout fortification and a more luxurious residence than some modern reconstructions suggest.[4] The 1562 drawing (see Plate 9) shows fine architectural features on the state buildings, including arcades of round-headed arches, decorated stone columns, ornate chimneys and roof finials. This quality was borne out by excavation, with finds of painted window glass (several examples of York's heraldic falcon, and a Virgin and Child presumably from the chapel); decorative masonry including gargoyles, one in the shape of a falcon; and decorative crests and finials from roof tiles.[5] Despite its grandeur, as many commentators have observed Sandal is a relatively small castle (nowhere near as big as the royal stronghold at Pontefract, for instance), measuring only 100m from the rear wall of the keep to that of the great hall, while the maximum diameter of the bailey is c.70m. It is impossible to know how many men could have fitted into its buildings (keep, barbican, gatehouse, constable's lodging, great hall, great chamber, chapel, kitchen, ancillary buildings) in such an emergency, but it was probably in the order of hundreds rather than thousands – and there would have been very little 'free' space between the buildings and moat in the bailey for others to camp. The bulk of York's troops must therefore have sought accommodation nearby, or camped in the deer-park or fields north of the castle.

The western/northern boundaries of the battlefield are delineated by the River Calder. In 1825, discoveries of human bones, spurs and fragments of swords and armour confirmed that the area north-west of the castle, now known as Portobello, formed part of the battlefield; sadly, the fate of these finds is largely unknown. One still extant is alleged to be an archer's sword, now in private ownership. Said to have been found during the cutting of a drain near Portobello House, it is a single edged 'hanger' of late medieval form with an unusual guard, somewhat resembling a weapon in the collections of the Royal Armouries.[6] Illustrations of the Wakefield sword[7] show it to be in surprisingly good condition for an excavated find, cleaned down to a shiny metallic original surface with a sharp edge and minimal pitting. Such excellent preservation is rare; archaeological ironwork from British sites is typically found heavily concreted, with the metal core partially or wholly converted to mineral corrosion products – as was the case with medieval and Civil War finds recovered from nearby excavations at Sandal Castle, and the spearhead discussed below. Unfortunately, no information survives regarding the burial context and soil conditions in which the sword was found, making it impossible to judge whether this is a *bona fide* example of pristine preservation or a Victorian fake. Its authenticity could be easily proved by radiography and metallographic analysis – but in the absence of such confirmation, it must remain open to question as a genuine battle relic. However, there is another archaeological find of known provenance from the same area: the iron spearhead shown in Plate 11, and now on display in Wakefield Museum.

Plate 11: Portobello spearhead. Photo © Wakefield Council.

The spearhead was a casual find made during the digging of foundations for the Portobello House Estate. Donated to the Museum in 1959, it is of typical late medieval form with an elongated leaf-shaped head, and entirely consistent with weapons in use at the time.

To the north of the battlefield, the chantry chapel still stands on the old bridge over the Calder named in the *Annales Rerum Anglicarum* as the place of Rutland's demise. Contrary to local opinion as related in Camden's *Britannia* of 1586, the chapel was not constructed by Edward IV in memory of the fallen, but can be more convincingly dated to the mid-14th century.[8]

Plate 12: The chantry chapel on Wakefield's medieval bridge

South of the bridge lies the area known as Fall Ings, its name suggesting that this was where the main rout took place as Yorkist troops fled towards Wakefield. As at Portobello, human bones and other artefacts are reported to have been found there in the 19th century – although again, their subsequent fate is unknown.

Within the area bounded by these features, another battle site is well attested: the location of the Duke's death near Sandal Castle. The site is mentioned in Gibson's 1722 extended edition of *Britannia* as 'a small square plot of land hedg'd in from a Close, within which (before the war between King Charles and the Parliament) there stood a cross of stone, where Richard Duke of York was slain.'[9] Clement Markham says the site was also marked by an ancient willow, the original cross having been destroyed during the Civil War. Indeed, local tradition describes York as having made his last stand by a clump of willow trees; this is not mentioned by contemporary sources, although plant remains from Sandal Castle confirm the presence of willow in the vicinity. The site appears on the 1850 Ordnance Survey map, described as the Duke of York's 'grave'; the stone monument that marks it today, in the grounds of a school on Manygates Lane, was erected in 1897 'by some who wish to preserve the traditional site'.

Nearby may also be the find spot of the earliest documented battle relic, described in *Britannia* as 'a large antique gold-ring… engraved in the characters of that age, *pour bon amour*; and on the out-side, which is very broad, are wrought the effigies of three saints'. The ring is mentioned in *Britannia*, by Markham and by J. W. Walker as forming part of the Thoresby collection in Leeds Museum, but like other finds from the battle, has since been lost.[10] Clearly a valuable, high-status object, the ring unfortunately bore no mark of ownership or any device to indicate whether it was a Yorkist or Lancastrian possession, although it must have been owned by one of the noblemen on the field.

Walker also illustrates the Wakefield sword and ring, together with three other finds allegedly from the battlefield.[11] One purports to be the Duke's signet ring, engraved with a crowned letter 'R'. The ring is said to have been found in 1653 and to have been in the possession of Archdeacon Grant of Rochester in 1865, but its whereabouts were unknown to Walker at the time of writing. Another is an early 15th century dagger with an ivy-root pommel, discovered in the river bed where it may have been dropped by a soldier fleeing the field. The third object, unearthed in 1760 near Sandal Castle, is an onyx seal exhibited to the Society of Antiquaries in 1763 by a Mr. Bartlet. The onyx is engraved with a helmeted soldier carrying a lance and leading a horse; its gold rim bears the damaged and highly enigmatic inscription *MANTICA MENTITUR IANVA NOSTOR EQVS*. This corresponds with the first half of a later notation jotted on an 11th – 12th century copy of a manuscript by Bede, held in Trinity College Library, Cambridge:

> *Mantica mentitur ianva nostor equvs*
> *Dives durus ego faciam gallina siligo*

Neither version makes much sense. The individual words mean *mantica*: a hand bag or portmanteau; *mentitur*: it is deceived; *ianua*: door; *nostor equs* (properly *noster equus*): our horse; *dives*: a rich man; *durus*: hard; *ego*: I am; *faciam*: I am made; *gallina*: chicken; and *siligo*: wheat, wheat flour. Apart from the verbs, all the words are in the nominative case and there is no grammatical construction or connection between them. In very poor Latin, it might be rendered as, 'A handbag; it is deceived, our horse at the door; I, ruthless rich man, I am made chicken flour.' It seems to be a list rather than a sentence, and the reason it should be chosen as a seal inscription is obscure.[12] However, it cannot be certainly identified as a Battle of Wakefield relic. The copying or re-use of classical *intaglios* for personal seals is known in England and France from the 11th – 12th centuries, consistent with the earliest building phases of Sandal Castle, and the nonsensical inscription and manuscript jotting could well originate from the incorrect copying of a Latin tag by someone unfamiliar with the language. Thus the seal might have been lost by a member of the Warenne family (the owners of the manor of Wakefield and builders of the castle) in the 12th to 13th centuries – or an heirloom handed down to one of the combatants at the battle. It seems unlikely that we will ever know.

Given the distribution of these actual and potential battle-related artefacts and the substantial number of people likely to have been involved, it is reasonable to assume that the Battle of Wakefield raged over the entire area from Sandal Castle in the south to the chantry chapel (or beyond) in the north, and bounded by the River Calder to the west. A final factor to bear in mind is that the distance between these points is quite small: little over a mile from Sandal Castle to Wakefield, and about nine miles from Wakefield to Pontefract.

Plate 13: From Speed's 1610 map of the West Riding of Yorkshire, showing Wakefield and its environs. The deer-park of Sir John Savile's seat at Thornhill can be seen to the west of Sandal Castle. Photo by Sally Mills; reproduced by kind permission of West Yorkshire Archive Service, Wakefield, ref. C559/76.

This has significant implications for troop movements prior to, and during, the engagement. For instance, depending on the weather, the condition of the roads and their degree of lading, Lancastrian soldiers could have marched from Pontefract in half a day, while any mounted Yorkist scouts watching the roads could have conveyed news of their departure within an hour. This would have left ample time for troops billeted in Wakefield and nearby hamlets to be summoned and make their way to Sandal Castle – a half hour's brisk march for pedestrians, even less for riders – which brings us to a consideration of the battle itself.

The Battle

The explanation of what really happened at Wakefield may be so obvious that it is frequently overlooked – an example of commentators being 'unable to see the wood for the trees'. So with the myths stripped away, what follows is a version of events consistent with the most reliable evidence, and which may edge closer to the truth of the encounter.

The key to the whole mystery lies in the *English Chronicle*, indirectly supported by the *Annales Rerum Anglicarum* and William Gregory, and later reiterated by John Stow. At some point before Christmas, the Duke of York was approached at Sandal Castle by John, Lord Neville, (the Earl of Westmorland's brother), requesting a commission of array to recruit on his behalf. The *Chronicle* says he came on Christmas Eve, although as some historians observe, even if the approach was made on 21st December (the earliest given date for York's arrival at Sandal), this would create an unrealistically tight time-frame to muster troops and march to Wakefield for a battle that took place on the 30th.[13] David Cooke is particularly sceptical regarding Neville's role, believing it to be the chroniclers' excuse for York's defeat and questioning how his reportedly large force could have been raised in such a short time. The logical response is that Neville had already gathered troops, both to molest the Duke's northern estates and in preparation for a devastating battle plan; requesting a commission of array was merely the bait for a Lancastrian trap, a 'failsafe' to lull York into a false sense of security and ensure his defeat. Naturally the Duke granted this request, as must have seemed perfectly reasonable. The Nevilles were after all his wife's family; Richard Neville, Earl of Salisbury, together with his sons John, Thomas, and Richard, Earl of Warwick, were among his staunchest supporters. Presumably York was greatly heartened by this promise of imminent assistance. Warwick and March might have been far from his aid, but this was no longer so important if he would have Lord Neville's muster swelling his ranks.

This development puts a very different complexion on the course of events. The Duke of York no longer appears as a passive victim who suddenly found himself besieged by enemies who had crept up on him unawares, thanks to his own poor management and the incompetence of his scouts. He did not foolishly sacrifice his mobility[14] but elected to await Neville's reinforcements in safety, obliging the Lancastrians to bring their troops to do battle on an excellent ground of his choosing (as it presumably appeared to him): the plain field between Sandal and Wakefield, bounded by the river, with a secure stronghold at his back. Unfortunately for York, he did not realise that this particular Neville had held firmly to his Lancastrian affinity. Gregory identifies him as one of the lords called to muster by Queen Margaret; and according to the *Annales Rerum Anglicarum*, Lord Neville had held council with the Earl of Northumberland and Lords Clifford and Dacre in York in November to plan their campaign of harassment against the Duke's northern tenants – when in all probability, they also hatched this plot of deception and betrayal.

If we surmise that Lord Neville was in regular contact with both York and the Lancastrian commanders in the run-up to battle, the so-called 'Christmas truce' can be seen in a new light – a necessary hiatus for him to complete the muster and travel to the field on a date anticipated as keenly by his true allies as it was by the Yorkists. Meanwhile the Duke, with Sir John Savile's aid, sent foraging parties out and scouts to watch the approaches from Pontefract; other troops were conceivably occupied in erecting defences around their camp and artillery positions. Then if we can believe Jean de Waurin, York was further cheered by the arrival of 400 'well indoctrinated' men sent by Andrew Trollope in the guise of supporters. Haigh is sceptical about this story, as none of the other chroniclers mention it, and de Waurin was compiling a largely pro-Yorkist history – maybe he invented it to illustrate Lancastrian perfidy.[15] Or it may be true; perhaps de Waurin, with his military connections, was party to some 'insider information' which other writers at the time failed to pick up.

Whatever the case, peace ended when the Lancastrians left Pontefract for Wakefield. The exact timing of their departure is a matter for conjecture. If they set out before 30th December, they faced the risk of billeting their troops for one or more nights in enemy territory; so conceivably, given the relatively short distance they had to travel, they did not depart until first light on the 30th, arriving at Wakefield and deploying on the battlefield as the morning wore on. Alternatively and arguably better supported by the sources, they left on Monday 29th. This could account for discrepancies regarding the battle's date and the references to foragers, inviting speculation that the Battle of Wakefield actually involved two separate encounters: an opportunistic attack on a foraging party by the advancing Lancastrians on the 29th, followed by the battle proper the next day. (The bloody aftermath at Pontefract on the 31st, when prisoners living and dead were beheaded, might have added to contemporary confusion as to exactly when the battle began and ended). Either way, on receiving news of his enemy's approach, York must have summoned his men billeted in the town and nearby, cramming as many as he could into and around Sandal Castle in a state of high alert.

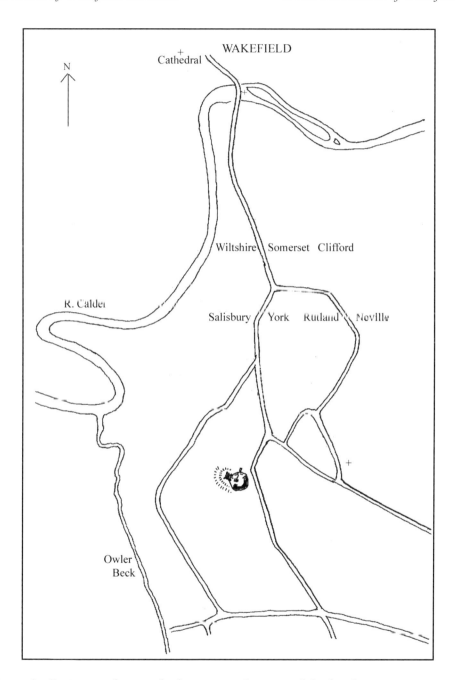

Figure 3: Conjectured troop deployment at the start of the battle

The eastern approach to Wakefield would have led the Lancastrian commanders to an obvious battleground. Possibly to the Duke's great satisfaction, their army took up position on the ridge of higher land just south of the town, with its right flank anchored by the River Calder; and there they waited, with their troops fully visible across the mile of open fields to Sandal Castle, ostentatiously cutting off communication between the castle and town. If any pre-battle parley took place, this would have been the time for it – although there was no room for compromise on either side. York's position could only be that the Lancastrians must submit to the Act of Accord; theirs that it must be overturned, ideally by the hated pretender's death. So if there *is* any grain of truth in the 'taunting heralds' tale, perhaps this is when it happened; Richard of York demanding acceptance as King Henry's rightful heir, and the Lancastrians retorting, in effect, 'come forth and make us'.

Whether the Lancastrians deployed at Wakefield on the 29th or 30th December, we do not know if the army they put on the field represented the entire force from Pontefract, or as Cooke suggests, their arrival was staggered in a ploy to deceive the Duke regarding their true strength. But their commanders including the Dukes of Somerset and Exeter, the Earls of Devon, Northumberland and Wiltshire, and the Lords Roos and Clifford, would have been supremely confident. They had a well-prepared strategy, far simpler, more reliable and less risky to their own men than trying to hide an ambush near Sandal Castle and goad York out with insults and harassment of his foragers; and unlike the Duke, they knew perfectly well what was coming.

What was coming - Lord Neville of course, with (according to the *English Chronicle*) 8,000 men; or if this is wild exaggeration, at least a substantial number. There is no record of the direction from which he approached, although if he had been recruiting in the Neville lands around Penrith and Raby it would have been from the north. He may have come through Wakefield itself, and fooled the Duke into thinking his enemy could be trapped in a pincer movement.[16] Equally he could have travelled down the Great North Road – maybe even calling at Pontefract to finalise details with his co-conspirators, then approaching, like the main army, from the east. Possibly Neville made rendezvous with the Duke at Sandal Castle, and marched to the battlefield with him; or (perhaps more likely) took his troops straight onto Wakefield Green and deployed them somewhere between the castle and the Lancastrian left flank (York's right). Whatever his manoeuvre, his arrival was anticipated and would have aroused no suspicion in the Yorkist camp – or opposition from the Lancastrians.

This was the moment York had been waiting for. With his own army swelled by Neville's contingent and 400 of Trollope's men, the odds looked much more attractive. He had no need to risk being besieged for weeks waiting for Edward and his troops, because reinforcements had already arrived. Furthermore, according to de Waurin, his morale was bolstered still further on the morning of the battle by the arrival of Andrew Trollope himself with more men, claiming (without introducing themselves) that they were coming to his aid. For Trollope to arrive *incognito* seems hardly credible, since he was such a prominent and well-known figure; perhaps more likely is that he did some convincing grovelling to be admitted. His excuse, which would have seemed plausible enough, was that he and the Calais contingent had not wished to stand against Henry VI at Ludford Bridge; whereas on this occasion, the Duke was fighting (nominally, at least) on the King's side, and at his behest.

Some historians believe that Trollope's troops approached in fake livery, pretending to be from the Earl of Warwick. This appears to be an over-interpretation of the evidence; de Waurin merely says that Trollope's men were to 'tell the duke that they were coming from Lancashire to rescue him' – implying that they were clad only in the false colour of friendship, rather than in counterfeit livery. Subscribers to the theory that these men were literally disguised do not stop to question how they might have *obtained* such fake livery, which must either have been illicitly procured or fabricated in the run-up to battle. In the days before mass-production, the making of even simple livery like sashes, tabards and badges would be no mean undertaking; moreover, the items would have had to be convincing enough to fool all Warwick's kinsmen in the Yorkist army. (Unfortunately for modern historians, Andrew Trollope did not survive to support or refute de Waurin's claims – he and his son David were both killed three months later, fighting for the Lancastrians at Towton).

Possibly York also believed, or was led to believe, that more Lancastrians would defect to his cause, just as he had expected them to support his claim to the throne in October. It is important to remember how any additional putative supporters would have appeared to the Duke: they were not only flocking to his banner but to the *King's*, York having been despatched to suppress northern insurrection with the full force of royal command and the backing of parliament. So it is worth re-stating that at this point, Queen Margaret and her adherents were the rebels and traitors - hence the Duke's lack of surprise or suspicion when Neville and Trollope apparently chose to obey King Henry's orders and rally to his side.

Irrespective of whether he still had foragers out scouring the country, York now felt his forces were sufficient to engage the enemy with every chance of success. And there we have the most obvious solution to the mystery of why the Duke rode out from Sandal Castle – not unreasonably, *he thought he was going to win.*

So Richard of York did not charge out pell-mell to rescue foragers, in wanton disregard of good advice, or (necessarily) in ignorance of enemy numbers. He, Salisbury and Rutland left Sandal Castle by its north gate and led their men down onto Wakefield Green in good order to join their 'ally' Lord Neville. Presumably they were in good heart, buoyed up by the righteousness of their cause and the presence of 'reinforcements', expecting an evenly-matched fight wherein Rutland might win glory in his first command. The location of the Duke and Earl's subsequent deaths suggest that York led the centre battle, with Rutland, accompanied by Robert Aspall, leading the van on his right; this leaves their other high-ranking peer, the Earl of Salisbury, as the likeliest contender for commanding the rearward on York's left. Facing them, if Halle's account can be trusted, was the Duke of Somerset in the main battle, with the Earl of Wiltshire and Lord Clifford in the 'stalls' or 'stoles'. Since Clifford's reported role as Rutland's nemesis on or near Wakefield Bridge places him to the north-east of the battlefield, consistent with him commanding the Lancastrian left, Halle's version leaves the Earl of Wiltshire leading the van with his right flank anchored on the Calder (but gives no indication of the placement of other luminaries like the Duke of Exeter, the Earls of Devon and Northumberland or Lord Roos).

However they had deployed on the field, this was also the moment the Lancastrians had been waiting for. When the Duke's entire army was exposed on 'the plain ground between his castle and the town of Wakefield' as Stow describes it, they gave the order to attack. There is no evidence that any parley took place, nor whether the engagement opened with the traditional archery exchange. Possibly not, if as de Waurin reports, Trollope's men opened hostilities on a pre-arranged signal. If the Lancastrians *did* deploy Trollope in this capacity, and if they did so in order to avoid or disrupt an archery exchange, it implies they knew that they were weaker in archers than the Yorkists; but assuming this attack actually happened its impact would have been stunning, possibly out of all proportion to the size of Trollope's force. The Yorkist troops, taken completely unawares by the enemy in their midst, may have sustained heavy losses because they were too shocked to defend themselves effectively. Panic, confusion and dismay would then have rippled out through the ranks as more men realised that battle had commenced - and in an unorthodox manner, contrary to the expectations with which they had taken to the field. *If* this happened, it would have been a dreadful moment with the potential to swing the result even without further intervention; in studies of later conflicts it has been observed that, 'Decisive battles almost always lead first to the psychological and then, as a result, the physical collapse of one side'.[17] Conceivably, the sudden shock of betrayal, the casualties sustained, and the confusion arising from the disruption to their battle-plan and private expectations, could have kick-started the process of the Yorkist rout.

But irrespective of whether Trollope's surprise attack took place, there was an infinitely worse and greater shock in store. At some pre-arranged moment the John Nevilles piled in, not for the white rose but for the red – just as the Lancastrian commanders had known they would, but which came as a ghastly revelation to York's army. This unforeseen and catastrophic development must have had enormous impact on the troops in terms of terror and demoralisation, thereby reducing their fighting ability even as the blood-lust of their adversaries, now assured of easy victory, was heightened. Instead of the evenly-matched battle they had expected, the Yorkists were now forced to fight – or flee – for their lives.

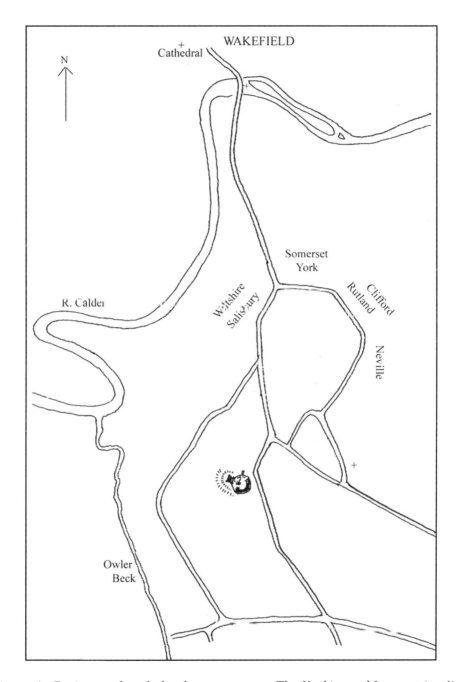

Figure 4: Conjectured early battle manoeuvres. The Yorkist and Lancastrian lines advance to meet each other while Lord Neville's force moves to flank Rutland.

Thus the odds were suddenly and hopelessly changed, particularly if Cooke's theory is correct and the Yorkist plight was compounded by the arrival of yet more Lancastrians: a paltry handful of thousands against a combined force possibly outnumbering them 3:1. And there we have the chroniclers' 'environing', from which so many have made so much: no complicated ambush, no hordes unfeasibly hidden behind mole-hills and trees, just a small army swallowed up by a much larger host – the Lancastrian centre straight ahead with the 'stoles' closing round, the Nevilles to York's right, the River Calder to his left and possibly the Trollopes infiltrated among the Yorkist line. If there *was* any form of flanking attack, rather than coming from the non-existent woods it may have involved a low hill in the Portobello area. This is clearly visible in the background of 19th century photographs of York's monument, inviting speculation that part of the Lancastrian van broke off, skirted the bank of the Calder out of the Yorkists' range of vision, and poured over this hill to assail them from the left; although even without such a manoeuvre, the result was a foregone conclusion.

Plate 14: The Duke of York's monument c. 1900, showing higher ground at Portobello. From the Eric Raper collection in the online archive of Wakefield District images, reproduced courtesy of <u>www.twixtaireandcalder.org.uk</u>.

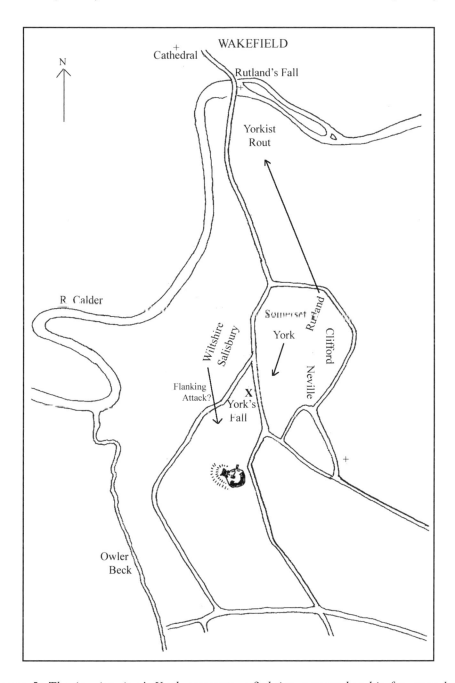

Figure 5: The 'environing'. York attempts a fighting retreat but his fate may have been sealed by a flanking attack around the hill in Portobello. Routing Yorkists break towards Wakefield but the Earl of Rutland is overtaken and killed.

Depending on their position on the field, some Yorkists (including the Duke) lacked the choice, and possibly the inclination, to do other than fight fiercely; those on the periphery may have begun to melt away. If Neville's troops and/or later Lancastrian arrivals *did* join the fray from the east side of Wakefield Green, the Yorkist line could have been split, squeezing Rutland's forces towards the bottle-neck killing field of Fall Ings, bounded to the east and west by a loop of the river – but also the path of escape towards Wakefield Bridge and the shelter of the town. York could not take this route; his only option was to attempt a fighting retreat, but he succumbed to sheer weight of numbers a heartbreakingly short distance from the safety of Sandal Castle. Assuming that the press of men between himself and his father was too great for the Earl of Rutland to follow suit, *his* only option was to fight or flee towards Wakefield; but he was overtaken and killed by Lord Clifford and his Flower of Craven either near the bridge chapel, or as some commentators believe, a short distance beyond it near a building called the Six Chimneys (since demolished) on Kirkgate.

Plate 15: An aerial view of Sandal Castle and the battlefield by Roger Keech, © RK Stills 2007.

Under the circumstances, the battle proper is unlikely to have lasted long, although the rout and pursuit may have continued for some hours. Edward Halle reports that the Duke of York, 'manfully fighting, was within half an hour slain and dead, and his whole army discomfited'; Polydore Vergil (albeit incorrectly attributing this to the encouragement of Queen Margaret) says that the residue of her enemies was vanquished 'in the moment of an hour'. Given the overwhelming superiority of Lancastrian numbers, we have no reason to doubt the essential veracity of these statements. The casualty figures are also believable under the circumstances, even Gregory's figure of 200 Lancastrians killed for more than ten times that number of Yorkists, when one considers the absolute terror and panic that must have swept through the latter's ranks as their doom became clear.

In conclusion, Richard of York was neither foolish nor an inept commander. He did not rush headlong from his stronghold goaded by pricks to his pride, outrage at Lancastrian truce-breaking, or in a misguided attempt to rescue a foraging party, oblivious to a hidden ambush – or at least, one that was physically hidden. This was no lunatic death-or-glory gambit, but a sensible military decision to engage an army of (ostensibly) roughly equivalent size, in the confident expectation of victory. In this respect the Duke was sadly deceived, but he should not be viewed as gullible or naïve because he fell for the enemy's ruse. In December 1460, York was King Henry's 'very dear cousin' and heir, acting upon a royal commission to subdue insurrection in the north (as well as protecting his own tenants and interests there). That his kinsman-by-marriage Lord Neville, possibly along with Andrew Trollope, a former Yorkist ally, should elect to fight on his side would have been completely plausible; and naturally the Duke would have *wished* to believe in their support, which could only have come as a great and joyful relief to someone in his position – a psychological chink in his armour the Lancastrians cunningly and deliberately exploited.

Notes

1. Dates of the battle, size of the armies and accounts of the action appear in the following sources referred to throughout the chapter: *Annales Rerum Anglicarum*, *op cit*, pp. 774 – 775; Gregory's *Chronicle*, *op cit*, p. 210; Vitellius AXVI, *Chronicles of London*, C.L. Kingsford (ed.), 1905, p. 172; Robert Fabyan's *The New Chronicles of England and France*, H. Ellis (ed.), 1811, pp. 637 – 638; *Great Chronicle of London*, A.H. Thomas and I.D. Thornley (eds.), 1938, p. 193; John Benet's Chronicle for the Years 1400 to 1462, *Camden Miscellany XXIV*, G.L. and M.A. Harriss (eds.), Camden Society, 1972, p. 228; *English Chronicle*, *op cit*, p. 107; Short English Chronicle, *Three Fifteenth Century Chronicles*, J. Gairdner (ed.), Camden Society, 1880, p. 76; Jean de Waurin, *Recuil des Chroniques d'Engleterre*, W. and E. Hardy (eds.), 1891, pp 324 – 326.
2. *Rotuli Parliamentorum*, 1st Edward IV (1461), vol. V, p. 477.
3. Malcolm Healey, 'Because it was winter?', *Towton Herald* (newsletter of the Towton Battlefield Society), Issue 47, Spring 2009, pp. 2 – 3.
4. See for instance the illustration in Haigh, *op cit*, p.23. Digital reconstructions of the castle buildings can be found on the DVD *Sandal*

Castle: The Battle of Wakefield 1460 & Building Sandal's Castles by John L. Fox, www.loyaltybindsme.com.

5. Mayes and Butler, *op cit,* 1983: L.A.S. Butler, 'Architectural Stonework', pp. 286 – 297, and 'Decorated Window Glass', pp. 318 – 321; S.A. Moorhouse, 'Pottery Roofing Material', pp. 308 – 316.

6. The Wakefield sword is described by G.M. Wilson, 'Notes on some early basket-hilted swords' in *Journal of the Arms and Armour Society*, 12 (1), March 1986, pp. 1 – 19; the Armouries weapon is illustrated in Rimer, *op cit*, p. 122.

7. Haigh, *op cit*, p. 94.

8. John W. Walker provides a detailed illustrated history and description of the chapel, suggesting it dates to the mid 1300's: 'St Mary's Chapel on Wakefield Bridge', *Yorkshire Archaeological Journal*, Vol 11, 1891, pp. 144 – 171.

9. *Britannia, or a Geographical Description of Great Britain and Ireland* by William Camden, 1586, revised by Edmund Gibson, 2nd edition, 1722, p. 856.

10. Markham, *op cit* p.114. The ring is illustrated in Haigh, *op cit*, p. 55, and J.W. Walker, *Wakefield, its History and People*, Vol. 1, S.R. Publishers Ltd., 3rd edition, 1966, p. 166.

11. *Ibid*, pp. 166 – 167.

12. A minimal description and drawing of the seal appear in *Archaeologia* Vol. VIII, p. 427 and Plate XXX, Fig. 1, and are reproduced in Walker (*ibid*). I am indebted to Lesley Boatwright of the Richard III Society and to David Rayner for their help in translating the inscription; also to David for tracking down the notation on the Trinity College manuscript. The coincidence of the wording on the seal and manuscript is mysterious, but Professor Richard Jameson of the University of Durham is confident that it has no connection with the writings of Bede. Was it a jokey piece of 'pig Latin', a mnemonic, or a coded expression commonplace at the time of writing whose meaning has since been lost?

13. Cooke, *op cit*, p. 106; Haigh, *op cit*, p. 40.

14. Miller, *op cit*, p.4.

15. Haigh, *op cit*, p. 64.

16. Haigh, *op cit*, p. 69.

17. Stephen D. Wesbrook, quoted in *Archaeology, History and Custer's Last Battle*, Richard Allan Fox Jr., University of Oklahoma Press, 1993, p. 39.

CHAPTER 5: THE FATE OF THE VANQUISHED

As previously discussed, it is impossible to be certain how many men fought or fell at the Battle of Wakefield. The best we can say is that a significant number of Yorkists died, while according to *Gregory's Chronicle*, the Lancastrians lost only 200 men (among whom were the son and grandson of William, Baron Bonville).[1]

Table 5.1: Yorkist Casualties of the Battle of Wakefield[2]

Name	Fate
Richard, Duke of York	Killed in battle, posthumously beheaded*
Edmund, Earl of Rutland	Executed, posthumously beheaded*
Richard, Earl of Salisbury	Captured and beheaded at Pontefract*
Captain John Baunne	Killed in battle
Sir Edward Bourchier	Killed in battle, posthumously beheaded*
Captain Roland Digby	Killed in battle
Captain Fitz-James	Killed in battle
Sir John Gedding	Killed in battle
Sir David Halle	Killed in battle
Captain Hanson	Captured and beheaded at Pontefract*
Sir Guy Harrington	Killed in battle
Sir Thomas Harrington	Killed in battle, posthumously beheaded*
Lord Harrington	Killed in battle
John Harrow	Captured and beheaded at Pontefract*
Sir Hugh Hastings	Killed in battle
Sir Ralph Hastings	Killed in battle
Walter Lymbrike	Captured and beheaded at Pontefract*
Sir Thomas Neville	Killed in battle, posthumously beheaded*
Sir John Parre	Killed in battle
Sir Thomas Parre	Killed in battle, posthumously beheaded*
Sir William Parre	Killed in battle
Sir James Pickering	Killed in battle, posthumously beheaded*
Sir Henry Ratford	Killed in battle
Captain Rathford	Killed in battle
Sir Ralph Stanley	Captured and beheaded at Pontefract*
Sir Eustace Wentworth	Killed in battle

* Denotes heads spiked on Mickelgate Bar and other gates of York.

95

So how did they die – and what happened afterwards, both to the slain and the survivors? Of the Yorkist high command, if we discount the 'Myth of the Ant-hill Throne' it seems most likely that Richard of York was overcome by weight of numbers as he tried to fight his way back to Sandal Castle, and his body posthumously dishonoured by decapitation the following day at Pontefract. The Earl of Rutland was executed by Lord Clifford; the Earl of Salisbury managed to escape only to be apprehended later and subsequently executed. Their fates, and those of other known Yorkist victims, are summarised in **Table 5.1**.

In the absence of human remains from the site, the manner in which those killed on the field met their deaths can only be conjectured by comparison with skeletons recovered from Towton. Since 1996, several mass graves have been excavated in and around Towton Hall, suggesting that these dead were originally interred in the hallowed ground of St Mary's church, the footprint of which has been subsumed within the present hall building. The injuries exhibited by the Towton casualties graphically illustrate what happened to the loser in medieval battles: multiple injuries, arrow strikes and blade cuts, broken and crushed bones from pole-arms and maces, and perforations from war-hammers or bills, often directed at the head.[3] Given that the same range of weapons and combat styles would have been used in both battles, we can surmise that the victims at Wakefield would have sustained a comparable range of wounds in the battle or rout.

What then became of the dead? In the case of York and Rutland, we have a substantial amount of historical detail: their bodies were buried in Pontefract, probably either at St Richard's Friary or the Priory of St John; reunited with their heads shortly after the Yorkist victory at Towton in 1461; exhumed in July 1476, and reburied with suitable pomp at York's castle of Fotheringhay.[4] It is reasonable to suppose that other captives later executed were also buried in Pontefract, either in the castle chapel or one of the town's religious houses.

The posthumous fate of other casualties is unknown. Some, particularly during the rout, may have been driven into the Calder and their bodies subsequently carried away down-river and lost or buried elsewhere. For the majority who fell on the field, given that the battle took place on farmland between centres of population, it is inconceivable that they were left to rot where they fell. Possibilities for their disposal therefore include:

- Burial in nearby sanctified ground, such as St Helens Church at Sandal Magna, or the precincts of Wakefield Cathedral
- Removal to their home parish for burial
- Removal to mass graves in Portobello, Fall Ings (evinced by 19th century finds of human bones) or other battlefield sites now inaccessible under later development
- Burial close to where they fell

Whatever the case, the impact on the local populace in the immediate aftermath of battle must have been considerable, with a field of corpses to clear and presumably, wounded to care for - because if we assume York's army numbered c. 5,000, the reported casualty figures mean that several thousand of his men escaped the slaughter. Their possible fates include:

- Missing the battle altogether (in the case of any absentee foragers, scouts or staff left at Sandal Castle)
- Escaping the field and successfully evading capture
- Escaping the field to be captured later and executed (like the Earl of Salisbury and other individuals listed in **Table 5.1**)
- Capture on the field and imprisonment in Pontefract or elsewhere
- Being disarmed and released, perhaps to subsequently die of their injuries
- Being absorbed into the Lancastrian army

However, some of York's army did live to fight another day:

Table 5.2: Yorkist Survivors of the Battle of Wakefield[5]

Name	Fate
John Neville, Baron Montagu	Survived Wakefield, captured at 2nd St Albans
Sir Thomas Burgh	Survived Wakefield and Towton
Sir Richard Hakluyt	Survived Wakefield and Towton
Sir John Melton	May have fought at Wakefield; died 1474
Sir Thomas Pickering	Captured if not killed
Sir John Plomer	Survived Wakefield, knighted after Towton
Sir William Rainford	Survived Wakefield and Towton
Sir John Savile	If fought, captured and imprisoned at York
Sir James Strangeways	Initially captured, survived Towton, died 1480
Sir Richard Strangeways	May have fought at Wakefield; died 1488
Sir William Stoner	Survived Wakefield and Towton
Sir Lancelot Threlkeld	Survived Wakefield and Towton
Sir Roger Vaughn	Survived Wakefield and Towton; executed 1472
Mr. Colt	Captured if not killed
John Woodruff	If fought, captured and imprisoned at York

Among them, Sir James Strangeways went on to fight at Towton; he then served Edward IV as speaker of parliament, and died in 1480. John Neville, Baron Montagu (the Earl of Salisbury's third son) survived Wakefield to be captured after the second Battle of St Albans; remaining loyal to his elder brother Richard, Earl of Warwick, was to cost him his life at Barnet in 1471. Sir John Savile and John

97

Woodruff, receiver of the lordship of Sandal, are likely to have taken part in the battle and evidence suggests they were captured: together with Baron Montagu, known to be held in York at that time, they witnessed a deed of enfeoffment dated 29th April 1461. Sir John's earlier support may be inferred by his family's continued prominence under Edward IV, and the office of Sheriff of Yorkshire awarded to him after Towton.[6]

The Fate of the Victors

Ostensibly, Wakefield was a great victory for Queen Margaret's cause and when news of it reached her, she must have rejoiced. Richard of York, that thorn in her side for so long, and the Earl of Rutland, third in line to the throne by the Act of Accord, had been eliminated together with many of their supporters. And apparently for very little cost; while contemporary chronicles mention numerous Lancastrian combatants at Wakefield, they do not list any casualties, suggesting their losses were slight.

Immediately after the battle the Lancastrians must have rounded up prisoners, dealt with their own dead and wounded, salvaged equipment from the field, and ransacked Sandal Castle and any adjacent Yorkist camp for items of value. A number of combatants were knighted for their service on the field (see **Table 5.3**), then the army, possibly swelled by erstwhile Yorkist troops, returned to Pontefract accompanied by live captives and the bodies of York and other prominent victims.

Margaret of Anjou's next priority was to 'liberate' her husband from Yorkist control, and her large army comprising the victors from Wakefield, levies from the northern shires and her new Scottish allies, duly marched south to the capital. However, they might have won the battle but the war was far from over; the blood-feud had merely been whipped up to an even greater degree of intensity, and a powerful new nemesis created. By his father's death Edward of March had become Duke of York and the new heir-apparent to Henry VI; and backed by a royal commission, it now fell to him to suppress the rebel Queen and her allies. It was a task Edward set about with a will, driven by a fierce desire to avenge his father and brother, and a need to safeguard the younger Yorkist princes George and Richard (shortly to become the Dukes of Clarence and Gloucester), who were sent to Burgundy in March out of harm's way.

Edward began his campaign of vengeance by defeating the Earls of Pembroke and Wiltshire at Mortimer's Cross in early February 1461, and the subsequent execution of captives including King Henry's father-in-law, Owen Tudor.[7] In the meantime Queen Margaret's underpaid forces pillaged their way down the Great North Road, plundering towns like Grantham, Peterborough and Huntingdon in lieu of pay, terrifying the population and losing support for their cause in the process. The *Crowland Chronicle, Whethamsted's Register* and the *English Chronicle* all give vivid accounts of the Lancastrians' 'execrable and abominable' behaviour on this march;[8] the Paston Letters also allude to them having been appointed to rob, steal, pillage and give away men's goods and livelihoods.[9]

Notwithstanding this lack of discipline they managed to defeat the Earl of Warwick, who rode out to meet them, at the Second Battle of St Albans on 17th February; since Warwick had not dared leave Henry VI behind in the capital, they also wrested the King back from his Yorkist custodians. But the Lancastrian victory was not decisive. Warwick and many of his troops escaped and subsequently linked up with Edward in the Cotswolds, while the King and Queen failed to capitalise on their opportunity to re-take London either by negotiation or force. The sources are somewhat confusing on this point; according to the *Annales Rerum Anglicarum*, Queen Margaret balked at letting her troops into the city because she could not guarantee they would not sack it, whereas the *English Chronicle* reports that the commons locked the gates against them after disposing of a small contingent sent by the Duke of Somerset.[10] Both explanations are credible. Margaret's Scottish and northern troops were probably fighting more for blood-lust and the promise of booty than loyalty to the Lancastrian crown, and it is easy to imagine London's panic-stricken populace refusing to admit such dangerous marauders, a combination of Yorkist propaganda and dire tidings of their activities *en route* to St Albans having done effective work. Additionally, there was much support for the immensely wealthy, generous and flamboyant Earl of Warwick; uncertainty over King Henry's title to the throne (thanks to York's claim and the Act of Accord); distaste for Queen Margaret's rebellion and its consequences; and doubtless in some quarters, great alarm at the prospect of the Lancastrian monarchs resuming their clumsy and partisan rule.

Whatever the truth, Margaret and Henry chose not to press the matter and their army withdrew to the north - leaving the way clear for the Yorkists to return. By this point, the new Duke of York had plainly arrived at the same conclusion as his father, and for similar reasons: with King Henry back in the hands of his wife and friends, Edward could expect no better treatment from the Lancastrian regime than the late Duke had received. Therefore he would no longer fight *for* the King – instead, for the sake of his future career and his family's security, he must *be* the King. So, perhaps taking a lesson from Duke Richard's unlucky attempt at a *fait accompli*, the new Yorkist claimant first gauged the reaction of several thousand Londoners at St John's Fields in late February. Meeting with success, he then summoned the citizens to watch him process from St Paul's to Westminster on 4th March, where he was enthusiastically accepted as King Edward IV.[11] Even allowing for the Yorkists' stage-management of events, the response was understandable. Edward's age (he was a month short of his 19th birthday) meant he could not be held accountable for English losses in France, mismanagement at home or the political upheavals of the 1450's; he promised to be a 'new broom', a fresh start for the realm. Moreover, the recent victor of Mortimer's Cross *looked* like a king: over six feet tall, athletic, handsome, (his nickname was the 'Rose of Rouen'), and much blessed with personal charm, he must have seemed like God's gift compared with the pleasant but insipid King Henry.

Thus England acquired a second king - whose formal coronation could not proceed until the first had been disposed of. So now it was Edward's turn to march north in an eerie echo of the Wakefield campaign: the royal army gathered around York, luring the Yorkists far from the capital and their southern power base, ready to crush them with an overwhelming (and perhaps over-confident) force. Initially it seemed the Lancastrians would succeed; the commanders chose an apparently excellent battle-ground on a ridge of high land just south of Towton, far enough from York for the royal family to await news of their victory in safety. Their troops were well fed and rested, while the Yorkists had faced a long forced march through bitter weather, and suffered casualties (including Lord Fitzwalter) as a result of Lord Clifford's spirited defence of the crossing at Ferrybridge. But Yorkist luck began changing the next day, when Clifford and his Flower of Craven were outflanked and slaughtered at Dintingdale before they could rejoin the main host; and even the wintry weather, which caused much suffering in the run-up to battle, acted in their favour. On Palm Sunday, 29th March 1461, the southerly wind and driving snow were exploited by canny Lord Fauconberg, who advanced his archers to send a deadly arrow-storm into the enemy ranks – arrows the Lancastrians, shooting into the wind, could not effectively return.

Fighting conditions at the Battle of Towton were horrible: poor visibility and slippery, snow-covered ground littered with spent arrows and corpses. Notwithstanding the early advantage they had gained in the artillery exchange, the Yorkists were gradually pressed back by weight of numbers – but in the nick of time, the day was saved by the Duke of Norfolk (who had been delayed at Pontefract, possibly by illness), bringing reinforcements. The arrival of fresh troops heartened the Yorkists as much as it dismayed their opponents, who began fleeing down the precipitous slopes from the Towton plateau to Cock Beck in what became the most calamitous and bloody rout of the whole Cousin's War. The beck, innocuous enough when the Lancastrians had taken up position, was now in full spate, swollen by snow-fall. Thousands of desperate men plunged in, and if they were not dispatched by the pursuing Yorkists, either drowned or succumbed to shock and hypothermia in the freezing water to pile up in grisly 'bridges of bodies'. Many more were ridden down as they broke towards Towton and Tadcaster, and by the end of the day, the death-toll could have exceeded 30,000. Among the dead were some of the regime's key supporters: the Lords Dacre, John Neville, Scales, Scrope, Welles, Willoughby and Morley, the Earl of Northumberland, and the redoubtable Andrew Trollope.

Table 5.3: Lancastrian Combatants at Wakefield: Peers[12]

Name	Fate
Henry Beaufort, Duke of Somerset	Executed after Battle of Hexham, 1464
Henry Holland, Duke of Exeter	Drowned at sea, 1475
Thomas Courtney, Earl of Devon	Injured at Towton, beheaded in April 1461
Henry Percy, Earl of Northumberland	Killed at Towton
James Butler, Earl of Wiltshire	Captured and executed in May 1461
John, Lord Clifford	Killed at Dintingdale
Ranulph, Lord Dacre of Gilsland	Killed at Towton, buried in Saxton
Henry, Lord Fitzhugh	Submitted to Edward IV after Towton
Ralph, Baron Greystoke	Career courtier, died 1487
Robert, Baron Hungerford	Captured and executed after Hexham, 1464
John, Lord Neville	Killed at Towton
Thomas, Lord Roos	Captured and executed after Hexham, 1464

Plate 16: The tomb of Ranulph, Lord Dacre of Gilsland, in Saxton churchyard; the pyramid on the right is the monument by sculptor Stephen Hines, commissioned by Towton Battlefield Society and erected in 2005 to commemorate the fallen.

Table 5.4: Lancastrian Combatants at Wakefield: Knights

Name	Fate
Sir Richard Aldborough	Knighted at Wakefield, fought at Towton
Sir Thomas Babthorpe	Knighted at Wakefield, fought at Towton
Sir Henry Bellingham	Knighted at Wakefield, fought at Towton
Sir William Bertram	Knighted at Wakefield, fought at Towton
Sir John Bigot	Killed at Towton
Sir Ralph Bigot	Killed at Towton
Sir Henry Bokeham	Killed at Towton
Sir John Butler	Fled to Ireland after Towton
Sir Rodger Clifford	Knighted at Wakefield, survived Towton, executed 1485
Sir Gervaise Clifton	Executed after Battle of Tewkesbury, 1471
Sir Thomas Everingham	Killed at Towton
Sir Baldwin Fulford	Survived Towton, later executed
Sir Thomas Fulford	Survived Towton, died 1490
Sir Thomas Fyndern	Among those attainted by Edward IV
Sir William Gascoigne	Knighted at Wakefield, fought at Towton
Sir Symond Hamomes	Among those attainted by Edward IV
Sir John Heron	Killed at Towton
Sir Alexander Hody	Knighted at Wakefield, fought at Towton
Sir William Holland	Killed at Towton
Sir Arnold Hungerford	Killed at Towton
Sir Nicholas Latimer	Knighted at Wakefield, survived Towton, died c. 1505
Sir Henry Lewes	Knighted at Wakefield, killed at Towton
Sir Anthony Notehill	Among those attainted by Edward IV
Sir John Maulever	Knighted at Wakefield, survived Towton, died 1476
Sir Thomas Metham	Knighted at Wakefield, fought at Towton
Sir Richard Percy	Knighted at Wakefield, killed at Towton
Sir William St Quyntin	Knighted at Wakefield, fought at Towton
Sir William Stapleton	Survived Towton, died 1503
Sir William Tailboys	Survived Towton, executed 1464
Sir Andrew Trollope	Killed at Towton
Sir Richard Tunstall	Captured at Harlech, 1468, died 1491
Sir Robert Whittingham	Knighted at Wakefield, killed 1471

As to the fate of lesser persons, it is said that at Towton, Edward did not issue the customary order to 'kill the nobles, spare the commons':

Table 5.5: Lancastrian Combatants at Wakefield: Gentlemen and Commoners

Name	Fate
Thomas Baron, Mason	Killed at Towton
John Botiller, Squire	Killed at Towton
John Caterall, Gentleman	Killed at Towton
John Clapham, Yeoman	Killed at Towton
John Crackenthorpe	Killed at Towton
Thomas Crackenthorpe	Killed at Towton
Henry Clyffe, Yeoman	Killed at Towton
James Dalton, Gentleman	Killed at Towton
Thomas Dalton, Gentleman	Killed at Towton
Thomas Frysell, Smith	Killed at Towton
William Typpes, Yeoman	Killed at Towton
William Grimsby, Squire	Killed at Towton
William Harill	Fatally wounded at Towton
Richard Hatecale, Yeoman	Killed at Towton
Gawen Lampleugh, Tailor	Killed at Towton
Richard Lister, Yeoman	Killed at Towton
Philip Lowes, Clerk	Killed at Towton
John Smothyng, Yeoman	Killed at Towton
David Trollope	Killed at Towton
Robert Tomlynson, Yeoman	Killed at Towton
Thomas Tunstall, Squire	Killed at Towton
John Welpdale, Clerk	Killed at Towton
Philip Wentworth	Survived Towton, executed 1464

The fortunes of Lancastrian survivors of Towton varied dramatically. Some, including Lord Roos and the Dukes of Exeter and Somerset, realised that the day was lost and escaped before they could be overtaken by the general rout. Riding to York they broke the dire news to Henry and Margaret, and all fled together into Scotland – where the Queen ceded Berwick, the price she had negotiated for Scottish aid. The Earl of Devon, Margaret's cousin-by-marriage, was too badly wounded to join their flight – or to evade the victorious Yorkists. He was beheaded at York on 3rd April; a month later, the Earl of Wiltshire, the rapacious treasurer who had rejected Richard of York's patronage, was captured and beheaded at Newcastle. However, Edward IV was willing to be magnanimous towards others like Ralph, Baron Greystoke, who had probably been drawn into the conflict with great reluctance. A career courtier apparently more concerned with working for the crown than with whose head it sat on, Greystoke submitted immediately after Towton, serving Edward and then his successors Richard III and Henry VII until his death in 1487.[13]

More surprisingly, Edward also reconciled with his father's bitter enemy Somerset, who had initially continued working for the Lancastrians. Despite their catastrophic losses and a new king triumphantly installed on his throne, the ousted Queen had refused to admit defeat and in July 1461, despatched Somerset to France to solicit funds and a fresh army from her uncle, Charles VII. Unluckily for them both, Charles had recently died and his successor, Louis XI, was a Yorkist sympathiser who promptly clapped the Duke in prison. After his release and removal to Burgundy thanks to intervention by the Count of Charolais, Somerset, isolated from his companions, apparently became disillusioned with their failing cause. By late 1462 he was negotiating with the Earl of Warwick; and in December, instead of helping Lancastrian rebels in Northumbria to hold out, he surrendered Bamburgh Castle to the Yorkists. Perhaps recognising his value as a commander, against all the odds King Edward granted Beaufort a full pardon in 1463, reversed his attainder, freed his younger brother Edmund from prison, and attempted to secure his loyalty with unusual marks of favour.[14]

Henry VI meanwhile remained in Scotland and Northumbria, nominally presiding over Lancastrian resistance, and Margaret established an impoverished small court in exile at her father's duchy of Bar[15] with her son and the Duke of Exeter sharing her vicissitudes. Somerset's defection from their cause proved to be short-lived; he was soon plotting again with Lancastrians in Wales and the north, where their rebellious forces were defeated in battles at Hedgeley Moor and Hexham in the spring of 1464. Spurned and betrayed, King Edward was not disposed to be merciful again; the Duke was beheaded at Hexham immediately after the battle on 15th May, with the Lords Hungerford and Roos sharing his fate a few days later at Newcastle. The Northumbrian castles of Alnwick and Dunstanborough then capitulated, although Harlech in Wales held out against the Yorkists until 1468. Henry himself went into hiding, sheltered by sympathisers in Lancashire, West Yorkshire and Westmorland. He was eventually captured near Clitheroe in July 1465, paraded through the streets of London, and subjected to a relatively benign incarceration in the Tower for the next five years.

This situation might have continued indefinitely had it not been for a peculiar and unforeseen development: a fatal rift between Edward IV and his erstwhile mentor and champion the Earl of Warwick. The deterioration in their relationship may be traced back to 1464, and Edward's clandestine wedding to the comparatively low-born Lancastrian widow, Elizabeth Woodville. Such a union was hardly fitting for the King of England; disapproved of by his family, derided in the courts of Europe, their love-match also made a mockery of Warwick's negotiations to broker a politically advantageous marriage to a suitable foreign princess. Nor was Edward disposed to be ruled by the Earl in other matters of high policy, or to forge closer kinship between them by allowing his brother George,

Duke of Clarence, to marry Warwick's daughter Isabel. Thus in yet another sad repetition of history, mighty subjects were alienated by the off-hand treatment of their king. Predictably, they joined forces in rebellion; George married Isabel regardless, and in 1469 they succeeded in capturing Edward and made a short-lived attempt to rule through him. Less predictably, when this strategy failed the Earl went to Margaret of Anjou in France, and undertook to depose the king he had helped to make in order to restore her husband to the throne.

Understandably (and doubtless with great enjoyment), Margaret at first obliged her former enemy to sweat and grovel - but Warwick's unexpected offer represented the pathway back to power and she could not refuse it, even cementing the deal by wedding Prince Edward to the Earl's younger daughter, Anne.[16] In 1470 the unlikely allies obliged Edward IV to flee to Burgundy with his brother Richard, Duke of Gloucester (later to become Anne Neville's second husband), and in October Henry VI was brought out of captivity for the crown to be replaced on his bewildered head. King Henry's so-called re-adeption lasted only until the Yorkist brothers returned in force in spring 1471, and fought two decisive battles in which the Earl of Warwick was killed at Barnet on 14th April, and the Lancastrian Prince of Wales, recently returned from France with his mother, at Tewkesbury on 4th May.

Edward duly reclaimed his throne, clapped Henry back in the Tower, and paraded Margaret (apprehended a few days after the Battle of Tewkesbury) through the streets of London like a trophy. He also had the Duke of Exeter, who had returned from his exile in France and been seriously wounded at Barnet, dragged from sanctuary and imprisoned.[17]

By now it must have been clear to the Yorkist regime that the Lancastrian threat, already weakened by the death in battle, or subsequent capture and execution of many of its principals, must be completely extinguished lest its indefatigable figurehead should somehow rise again. And so on the night of 21st May 1471, in a very timely manner for the Yorkists, the deposed king died in prison. The official line was that Henry VI had died of melancholy over the loss of his son and crown; and given the well-known fragility of his mental condition, the claim is not as preposterously unbelievable as it might otherwise seem. However, the death was so convenient, and so essential for the regime's future security, it seems that on this occasion Edward IV *had* learnt a lesson from history. He was well aware that the former queen in particular would remain a focus for plots - especially while she was still theoretically capable of bearing another son if reunited with her husband (Margaret was by now in her early forties) - and the threat of further restoration attempts would overhang the House of York for the rest of Henry's life. So under these circumstances, the unofficial accounts are more likely to be true: that Henry VI was bludgeoned to death, possibly while kneeling at prayer, in a considered act of regicide ordered by King Edward. Indeed, when his remains were examined in 1910, remnants of (allegedly) blood-matted hair were found, consistent with a fatal blow to the head.[18] However, the reliability of these findings is open to question; examinations conducted before the advent of modern forensic techniques can be highly subjective, as shown by the lamentably biased 1933 study of the inurned remains in Westminster Abbey, popularly believed to be the sons of Edward IV.[19] Therefore to establish Henry VI's cause of death with greater certainty, his remains would need to be re-examined; sadly, as with the bones attributed to the 'Little Princes', there seems no imminent possibility of this happening.

But whatever the truth of the matter, by the death of Henry VI, Margaret of Anjou's extraordinary power was instantly and effectively neutralised. Bereft of both husband and son, she could make no independent claim to the English throne – and had no-one left to support her in any case. Initially the sorrowing widow was kept under close confinement then, possibly by the intercession of Queen Elizabeth, sent to live with her friend the Duchess of Suffolk. There Margaret remained until 1476, when she was ransomed by her cousin Louis XI, and spent the rest of her 52 years as his pensioner at the Chateau de Dampierre[20] – a sad and ignominious end for the most remarkable queen in medieval England.

Notes

1. Martin Cherry, 'Bonville, William, first Baron Bonville (1392–1461)', *Oxford Dictionary of National Biography*, Oxford University Press, Sept 2004; online edition, Jan 2008.
2. Combatants featured in the table are drawn from Appendices III and IV in Haigh, *op cit*, pp. 143 – 151, and *From Knights to Squires: The Gentry & Peerage of Towton*, Volume 1, Graham A. Darbyshire, Freezywater Publications, 2008.
3. See Fiorato et al, *op cit*, especially Chapter 8, 'Battle-related Trauma', pp. 90 – 102, and 'Case Studies', pp. 240 – 268, both by Shannon Novak.
4. Anne F. Sutton and Livia Visser-Fuchs with P.W. Hammond, *The Reburial of Richard Duke of York 21 – 30 July 1476*, The Richard III Society, 1996; see Note 9, p. 43, for a discussion of their original burial site.
5. Sources for the survivors listed are Darbyshire, *op cit*, 2008, and Clement Paston to John Paston, 23rd January 1461, in Gairdner, *op cit*, pp. 540 – 541.
6. See 'History of the Savile Family' adapted from a dissertation by Adam Woodland, on the website www.savilehousehold.co.uk.
7. An account of the battle of Mortimer's Cross can be found in Boardman, *op cit*, pp. 34 – 38.
8. Summarised in Dockray, *op cit*, 2000, pp. 106 – 107.
9. Clement Paston to John Paston, cited in Note 5 above.

10. Dockray, *op cit*, 2000, pp. 108 – 111.

11. Wolffe, *op cit*, pp. 330 – 331.

12. The sources for **Tables 5.3 - 5.5** are Haigh, *op cit*, pp. 143 – 151, and Darbyshire, *op cit*, 2008.

13. Keith Dockray, 'Greystoke family (*per.* 1321–1487)', *Oxford Dictionary of National Biography*, Oxford University Press, online edition, 2004

14. Michael K. Jones, 'Beaufort, Henry, second duke of Somerset (1436–1464)', *Oxford Dictionary of National Biography*, Oxford University Press, online edition, January 2008.

15. Maurer, *op cit*, p. 205.

16. *Ibid*, p. 207.

17. Perhaps balking at having his brother-in-law executed, Edward subsequently forgave Holland and allowed him to join the invasion of France in 1475, but on the return journey he drowned after falling (or being pushed) overboard – Hicks, *op cit*, 2004.

18. W.H. St John Hope, 'The Discovery of the Remains of Henry VI in St George's Chapel, Windsor Castle', *Archaeologia*, Vol. 62 (1911), pp. 533 – 542.

19. The examination by Lawrence Tanner and William Wright, 'Recent Investigations regarding the Fate of the Princes in the Tower', *Archaeologia*, Vol. 84 (1935), pp. 1 – 26, was grossly subjective and manipulated the evidence to 'prove' the bones belonged to Princes Edward and Richard. Their findings were comprehensively demolished by P.W. Hammond and W.J. White in 'The Sons of Edward IV: a Re-examination of the Evidence on their Deaths and on the Bones in Westminster Abbey', in P.W. Hammond (ed.), *Loyalty, Lordship and the Law*, Richard III Society, 1986, pp. 121 – 170.

20. Maurer, *op cit*, p. 208.

CHAPTER 6: FINDING PROOF POSITIVE

The preceding chapters give only theoretical solutions to the many questions posed by the Wakefield campaign. Before more definitive answers can be reached, a good deal of additional evidence is required; the following chapter outlines what that evidence consists of, and how it might be obtained.

Historical Evidence

The vast bulk of what we know, or think we know, about Wakefield is derived from documentary sources. These are enormously important records of how people at the time – court officials, chroniclers and correspondents like the Paston family and Francesco Coppini – perceived events; nonetheless, relying solely upon them to get at the 'truth' of York's ill-fated campaign is fraught with complications. No two individuals reporting on the same event do so in exactly the same way; their accounts are coloured by personal perspectives and bias, and the quantity and quality of information at their disposal. Unfortunately, we have no eye-witness reports of the Duke's march north, or the actions at Worksop and Wakefield, from either Yorkist or Lancastrian survivors. Thus the contemporary chronicles and newsletters are at least second-hand, with all the potential for distortion that implies. They are riddled with contradictions and ambiguities regarding even the simplest facts (like the date the battle took place), and at this distance in time, it is impossible to ascertain which is the most accurate. The difficulty is compounded by 15th century and later copying and translation of original documents; each time a source is reproduced, re-translated, reinterpreted, paraphrased or partially quoted, a new possibility for error or misunderstanding creeps in – as seen in the different versions of the *Annales Rerum Anglicarum* discussed in **Chapter 3**.[1] (To fully compare and contrast the primary sources relating to Wakefield, the numerous different reproductions and translations thereof, and the various interpretations placed on them by later historians, would make a book in itself; sadly, it is beyond the scope of the present work).

Notwithstanding these limitations, any fresh scrap of historical evidence pertaining directly or indirectly to the encounters at Worksop and Wakefield would be valuable and it may well exist, lying as yet undiscovered or unrecognised in archive collections. After all, Dr. Michael Jones unexpectedly came upon a reference in the cathedral records at Rouen, suggesting that Richard of York was absent on the Pontoise campaign at the time of his eldest son's conception – a discovery used by the popular historian Tony Robinson to develop the argument that Edward IV was illegitimate, and to construct a new royal genealogy based on descent from Margaret, Countess of Salisbury (the daughter of Edward's younger brother George, Duke of Clarence).[2] So we cannot discount the possibility that other relevant contemporary references have survived and may one day be found; however, unless and until this happens, archaeological fieldwork and research are more reliable and accessible methods of further illuminating the issues.

Archaeological Evidence

It has been observed that:

'Working out the most intricate details of past battles is a trying experience...Sorting battles chronologically, linking events and getting at the how and why questions are difficult propositions for the [...] historian. In the end, recollections of the event seldom jibe... Archaeology helps surmount such dilemmas if only because material remains and their patterns are not produced by someone's imperfect recall, not to mention biased recollections. I do not propose that archaeology serves up all the answers to various questions unanswerable through historiography. But perspectives from the ground prove indispensable when poring through the documents.'[3]

Archaeology has certainly proved invaluable in elucidating details of Wars of the Roses battles. Excavations in and around Towton have provided a wealth of information on the men who fought there,[4] and fieldwork is currently making a great contribution to the advancement of knowledge regarding the course and location of the Battle of Bosworth.[5] With respect to the Battle of Wakefield, archaeological investigations have the potential to uncover new evidence in a variety of ways:

- Desk-based research is the starting point to identify likely sites for closer investigation. Sources of information include historic maps; aerial photographs (including the Cambridge University collection); stray finds reported to the Sites and Monuments Record (SMR) or National Monuments Record (NMR); records of the Portable Antiquities Scheme, established to record finds made by metal detecting; the Yorkshire Archaeological Society's review of antiquarian accounts for the building of various estates, and reports of early fieldwork featured in the Society's journal archive; and the corpus of unpublished archaeological reports held by the SMR and local archaeology units.

- In the field, geophysical surveys which measure variations in the Earth's magnetic field (magnetometry) or electrical resistance in the soil (resistivity) could be undertaken to detect buried features on sites of interest identified by desk-based research.[6] (Resistivity surveys are expensive and if carried out, tend to be targeted on magnetometer results).

- Environmental archaeology (soil sampling and analysis of floral and faunal remains) could supplement map and documentary evidence to help reconstruct the medieval landscape – essential for considering the likely movements of armies and their deployment on the battlefield.[7]

- Metal-detector surveys in areas of interest could pinpoint buried ferrous and non-ferrous artefacts; a distribution plot showing concentrations of metal finds might indicate sites of military activity. However, a survey alone could not differentiate between Wars of the Roses metalwork and objects from different periods (including modern discards); to obtain such a level of information the survey would need to be followed by artefact recovery, with due consideration given to the necessary post-excavation analysis and care of finds.

- If justified by the results of research and field surveys (and/or by threats to the site), test pits, trial trenches or wider areas could be excavated to identify and record buried features and artefacts.

Archaeology could also help to answer such questions as:

- Where, and how big, was the 'Battle' of Worksop? Topographic and place-name studies might reveal features like ditches, head-dykes and areas of boggy ground or other vegetation which could have affected troop movements *en route* to the encounter, and highlight the likeliest river crossing-points. Further investigations in these areas might turn up military finds like arrowheads, weapon fragments, harness fittings and spurs, to confirm the *Annales* and help pinpoint the location of the clash; a large concentration of finds or the discovery of battle graves might give some indication of its magnitude. However, if Worksop was a limited encounter, it may have left very little evidence in the ground; usable equipment would almost certainly have been scavenged either by the Lancastrians or Yorkists, and bodies may have been removed to consecrated ground for burial.

- What routes did the armies take to the battlefield? Studying historic maps and itineraries, place-names, stray finds, field systems and aerial photographs (which might show roads and tracks as crop-marks, soil-marks or earthworks), would help to build up a picture of 15th century settlement patterns and the most direct or practical routes from A to B.[8] Trial-trenching along these routes could turn up finds indicative of the mass movement of men and horses (horse-shoes and nails, hob-nails, harness fittings and so forth); environmental analysis would indicate the type of vegetation and/or tree cover present. Such information would greatly assist in reconstructing the probable routes for the approach of Somerset and York's armies to the clash at Worksop, their subsequent journeys to Pontefract and Sandal Castles, and the approach of the main Lancastrian army to Wakefield. The latter would be particularly important for testing the theory of Knowles and Cooke that the Lancastrians deliberately took advantage of landscape screening *en route* to Wakefield.

- Was there a Yorkist camp at Sandal Castle? One obvious area for 'over-spill accommodation' for troops is the area of flat land to its immediate north (which was not investigated during the excavations at the castle proper). Geophysical surveys on this land might confirm the presence or absence of outlying buildings, or features such as post-holes and latrine or fire pits indicative of a temporary encampment. (Although such surveys can reveal the presence of sub-soil anomalies, they cannot determine which are man-made and which are natural geological features; this could only be done by excavating trial trenches on the anomalies). Latrine and/or rubbish pits would be particularly valuable finds, as excavation of their contents can provide a wealth of information: for example, food remains such as bones, seeds and shells, and coprolites (preserved faeces) give conclusive proof of the foodstuffs available to at least some of the troops at the time. In conjunction, a systematic programme of metal-detecting and artefact recovery could turn up a range of material indicative of an army camp: horse-shoes, nails, harness, armour or weaponry fragments, clothes fasteners and lace-ends, coins, knife blades and so on. The extent and distribution of any remains could confirm whether or not a proportion of York's army did camp at the gates of Sandal Castle, and might offer some clues as to its size and disposition.

- Where was the woodland around Sandal Castle? Environmental analysis could be used to support or refute the controversial 'men in the woods' theory, by resolving the question of whether such convenient wooded hiding places ever existed. Environmental specialists would be required to devise the sampling strategy, taking into account factors like prevailing winds and pollen 'sinks' to identify the best locations to test the hypothesis, and also to analyse the results. Soil samples could then be collected from areas like the open land to the south and west of Sandal Castle (the likeliest location for the documented deer-park); from the field to the north, to determine whether the castle was completely encircled by its park; and from the south bank of the River Calder to show whether the Portobello area was wooded at this time. Analysis of the pollen, insect and snail shell remains (from open land or shade-loving species) would indicate the flora and fauna present, and could be used to reconstruct the 15th century landscape and degree of tree cover. Such investigations could be supplemented by magnetometer surveys to search for lines of post-holes corresponding with the fence of the 'well-paled' deer-park. A search for occupation traces could also show whether the park was used as a camp-site or an area to corral horses which could not be stabled elsewhere.

- Has any further evidence of the battlefield (human remains, artefacts or features like buried earthworks, ditches, stakes or stake-holes) survived? This question might be answered by a 'Big Dig' community archaeology project to open up one-metre-square test pits in the gardens of the Portobello estate and on Manygates Lane. Any objects or human remains uncovered might enhance our understanding of the course of the battle; for instance, concentrations of arrowheads would indicate whether or not an archery exchange took place; finds of lead shot or gun fragments would confirm the presence of artillery; heraldic badges might pinpoint the position of known combatants on the field of battle. Traces of post holes, ditches, revetments and so on could indicate the position of battle-lines, the nature of the engagement and the extent to which preparations had been made in the field. Other features, like evidence of ploughing or agricultural finds, could shed light on the condition and use of the field prior to the arrival of troops.

Computerised Reconstructions

Ultimately, any new data obtained on the 15th century landscape, settlement pattern, road and path network, and finds (structures, artefacts or human remains) indicative of military activity could be synthesised into a computer model on which various theories could be tested – albeit by specialist operators and at enormous cost. A software package accurate enough to produce meaningful results is called 'Key TerraFirma'; this generates a visual envelope in the form of a polygon showing all the land visible from a selected view point (or collection of viewpoints), enabling the operator to add features like woods and buildings and to animate fly-throughs of the landscape. Results from the 1964 – 73 excavation project would allow an accurate scale model of Sandal Castle to be reconstructed and placed into this virtual 15th century landscape using GIS software (archaeological plans, sections and find-spots could also be plotted in). Lines of sight from the castle could then be extrapolated to support or refute the contention that Lancastrian forces made a covert approach shielded by landscape features. Bodies of virtual soldiers at the requisite scale could then be manipulated within the terrain to show how they would 'fit' in the landscape, and to develop models of how armies of various sizes might have moved and deployed on the Wakefield battleground.

In conclusion, archaeological evidence which could enhance our understanding of the Battle of Wakefield almost certainly does exist and could be recovered, but the process of doing so would be expensive and time-consuming. Archaeological investigations are typically driven by necessity in the face of building developments or change of land use, and archaeologists seldom enjoy the luxury of pursuing research purely to answer historical questions. However, the Wakefield campaign provides fertile ground for desk-based projects, and students of history or archaeology may one day choose to pick up some of the research threads outlined in this chapter. In the interests of historical accuracy, and for the sake of Richard of York and the many others who died in this battle, I hope so; I am not so attached to any of the theories presented in this book that I would not gladly revise them in the light of new discoveries from archival or field investigations.

Notes

1. See Chapter 3, Note 4. As well as these versions, translations of the *Annales* can be found in *England under the Yorkists* I.D. Thornley (ed.), 1920, pp. 8 – 9, and *English Historical Documents*, Vol. 4, 1327 – 1485, A.R. Myers (ed.), 1969, pp. 285 – 6.
2. Arguments in support of Edward IV's illegitimacy can be found in Jones, *op cit*, and developed in 'Britain's Real Monarch', a Channel 4 documentary produced in 2003.
3. Here, Richard Allan Fox, Jr. (*op cit*, p. 63) is discussing the archaeological evidence for Custer's famous 'Last Stand' at the Little Big Horn in 1876, although his remarks could equally be applied to the study of Wars of the Roses battles.
4. See Fiorato et al, *op cit*; also *The Towton Mass Grave Project*, T.L. Sutherland, www.brad.ac.uk/acad/archsci/depart/resgrp/towton and *The Towton Battlefield Archaeological Survey Project: an integrated approach to battlefield archaeology* by T.L. Sutherland and A. Schmidt, www.staff.brad.ac.uk/aschmidt/personal/Towton03-Preprint.pdf.
5. See 'Finding Bosworth', Glenn Foard, *Battlefield, Magazine of the Battlefields Trust*, Vol. 14, Issue 4, Winter 2009/10, pp. 9 – 13.

6. See M.S. Tite, *Methods of Physical Examination in Archaeology*, Seminar Press, 1972, especially Chapter 2, 'Location', for details of methodology.

7. John G. Evans, *An Introduction to Environmental Archaeology*, Elek Books Ltd. 1978, gives an excellent overview of the subject; *Plants and Archaeology* by Geoffrey Dimbleby, Paladin, 1978, provides further details of the preservation and analysis of plant remains from archaeological contexts.

8. See Michael Aston, *Interpreting the Landscape: Landscape Archaeology and Local History*, Routledge, 2000, especially Chapter 11, 'Communications – the Links Between'. *Maps for Historians*, Paul Hindle, Phillimore & Co Ltd., 1998, provides an extremely useful introduction to historical maps and their uses. Hindle, *op cit*, 1998 and *Roman Roads in Britain*, Hugh Davies, Shire Publications Ltd., 2008, are excellent brief guides to ancient road systems.

CHAPTER 7: A NURSERY RHYME DUKE?

Oh, the Grand Old Duke of York,
He had ten thousand men,
He marched them up to the top of the hill
And he marched them down again.
And when they were up they were up,
And when they were down they were down,
And when they were only half way up
They were neither up nor down.

This well-known rhyme is commonly thought to relate to Richard of York and his defeat at Wakefield. Whether or not this is likely to be true, or simply another misconception, is explored in the following chapter.

Nursery rhymes have been called 'the happy heritage of oral tradition'; they are songs or poems taught to young children to assist the development of vocabulary, counting skills (for instance *One, two, three, four five, once I caught a fish alive*), and co-ordination when the rhyme has associated actions or dances.[1] Some have ancient roots, and one which may have been familiar to protagonists at Wakefield features in a medical work by William Worcester dated to c. 1450. The joke is that it sounds like Latin when spoken quickly:

In fir tar is,
In oak none is,
In mud ells is,
In clay none is.
Can a mare eat oats?[2]

The best-known English nursery rhymes date from the 17th century onwards and often, like 'The Grand Old Duke of York', seem to originate in historical or political events - although the precise source and date of this verse, deriding a vacillating military commander, are debatable. Its present form, and the variant, 'The Brave Old Duke of York', can be traced back at least to the second half of the 19th century, but its antecedents may be much earlier. A very similar rhyme, 'The King of France & 4,000 men, They drew their swords and put them up again' has been known since the early 1600's, along with several other versions including:

The King of France went up the hill
With forty thousand men

117

> *The King of France came down the hill*
> *And ne'er went up again*[3]

As discussed in preceding chapters, it is highly unlikely that Duke Richard had anywhere near 10,000 men with him at the battle, (although this figure is mentioned by Jean de Waurin and later used by Shakespeare in Henry VI, which may account for the popular belief). Alternatively, it may have been adopted simply as a convenient round number which scans well with the verse.

Somewhat more accurately, as a member of the royal House of York and one of England's premier magnates, the Duke was certainly 'grand' and he was of mature years, albeit still vigorous enough at 49 to lead his troops into battle. By 15th century standards this would be considered a good age, though not necessarily 'old'; it was not unusual for people to live much longer, and indeed his widow, Duchess Cecily, survived until she was 80. Other possible interpretations are that 'old' means 'of olden days', rather than relating to an elderly duke *per se*; or that it is employed in an ironical or affectionate sense ('old chap'). Furthermore, Duke Richard could be said to have marched his men 'to the top of the hill' to Sandal Castle before Christmas 1460, and 'marched them down again' to do battle on Wakefield Green on 30th December.

The remainder of the verse can be viewed either as indisputable fact (up is indeed up, down is down, and half-way is neither one nor the other); a piece of irrelevant nonsense bearing no relationship to the course of events; or an imputation of indecisiveness which does not seem applicable to what is known of the Duke's conduct on this occasion. Altogether, the association is not particularly convincing; although if the rhyme *does* refer to Richard Plantagenet, it possibly originated in the Tudor period when it would have been amusing, even politic, to denigrate the Duke of York in such a fashion.

But if it does not relate to Richard of York, who else might be the subject of its mild lampooning? A closer examination of other historical Dukes of York may help to answer this question.

The Dukes of York

The first Duke of York was Edmund of Langley, the fourth surviving son of Edward III, who held the title from its creation until his death in 1402. In 1367, Prince Edmund accompanied his elder brother the 'Black Prince' on a successful mission to Spain, and was also involved in several expeditions into France in the 1370's, albeit without a significant commanding role. His single experience of major command was an expensive and embarrassing failure: taking an army to help the Portuguese attack Spanish Castile in 1381, which due to his un-enterprising leadership, resulted in a winter of stalemate followed by an ignominious peace treaty in 1382. In general, Edmund seems to have had little aptitude for warfare; he was described by the contemporary commentator Froissart as '*mol et simple et paisable*' (indolent, guileless and peaceable), while the later chronicler John Harding observed, 'When all the lords to councell and parlyment went, he wolde to hunte and also to hawking.'[4]

On the death of this reluctant soldier the title passed to his son Edward of Langley, a favourite of Richard II. Some successful military campaigning with King Richard in Ireland pre-dates the second duke's inheritance of the title, and he was also involved in campaigns in Wales and Burgundy under Henry IV. As a military leader, Edward seems to have inspired confidence in both the kings he served, being appointed (among other high offices) Admiral of England by Richard II, and Lieutenant of South Wales by Henry IV. He also commanded the right wing at the Battle of Agincourt, where he was killed in 1415[5] – and since he died childless, the title passed to his nephew Richard, son of the executed third Earl of Cambridge and our earliest popular contender to be the 'Grand Old Duke'.

Following Duke Richard's death at Wakefield his eldest son inherited the title, which subsequently merged with the Crown of England when this fourth Duke of York took the throne as Edward IV. It is therefore extremely improbable that the rhyme could refer to Edward, the 'Rose of Rouen', a skilful commander who was undefeated on the battlefield in his attempts to seize the crown from Henry VI in 1461, and again after the 're-adeption' ten years later – more a 'Grand King Ned' than a 'Grand Old Duke'.

In 1474 King Edward gave the dukedom to his eldest son, Richard of Shrewsbury. Sadly, the fifth duke had scant opportunity to become grand or old; he either died as one of the 'Little Princes in the Tower', or was spirited away into obscurity during the reign of Richard III, so cannot be the subject of the rhyme.

The title then became extinct until 1494 when it was conferred on Prince Henry, the second son of Henry VII. This Duke of York was too young to prove himself in battle during the last throes of the Wars of the Roses, which continued for some years after his father's accession. Following the death of his elder brother Arthur he was created Prince of Wales, duly succeeding in 1509 as Henry VIII when the title merged once more with the Crown. The many surviving images of Henry show him to have been grand indeed, both in stature and adornments, although he is far better known for his marital than his martial exploits and remembered as 'Bluff King Hal' rather than as a Duke of York.

The next title-holder was Charles Stuart, second son of James I, who became Prince of Wales in 1616 after the death of his elder brother. As Duke of York, Charles indicated his readiness to fight against Spain, but England's various plans for a Continental war never came to fruition largely due to the diplomacy of King James. In 1625, aged 25, he came to the throne as Charles I whereupon the title merged again with the Crown. This makes him another unlikely candidate as the nursery rhyme's subject, notwithstanding his various military reversals against

France and Spain in the late 1620's, and against Parliamentary forces in the English Civil War of the 1640's.[6]

His son James Stuart, styled Duke of York from his birth in 1633 and one of the most actively militaristic holders of the title, is perhaps a more likely contender. As a member of the Stuart court in exile, James opted for a military career and joined the French army at the age of 19. He acquitted himself so ably in the Franco-Spanish War that he was promoted to Lieutenant-General, although in 1657, at the insistence of his brother Charles II, he was obliged to switch his allegiance to Spain.[7] Throughout, Duke James recorded his military experiences in a detailed memoir[8] which reveals that hills featured in a number of the actions he took part in (hardly surprising, given the strategic value of high ground). One of the most notably hilly was the battle for Dunkirk in 1658, also known as the Battle of the Dunes. There, Duke James and the Spanish forces were defending a 50-metre high sand-hill down which he led several cavalry charges, only to be repulsed by the French. Like his predecessors, this Duke of York could fairly be described as 'grand'; on this occasion he did have approximately 10,000 men under his command; he did march (or gallop) them up and down a hill; and despite his best endeavours, Dunkirk was lost to the French. On the other hand he was certainly not old; and far from the futility and indecision implied by the nursery rhyme, his memoirs and the favourable reports of contemporaries show James to have been a dynamic, capable and courageous leader, often found in the thick of battle.

The eighth Duke of York's military career continued during the Restoration. He was appointed Lord High Admiral of England in 1660, in which capacity he saw active service in the Anglo-Dutch Wars. His last sea-battle was the Battle of Southwold Bay in 1672, after which Charles II, in concern for his safety, forbade him to continue. Three years later he succeeded as James II and again the title merged with the Crown, only to come into dispute as a result of his conversion to Catholicism which made English Protestants unwilling to accept James Francis Edward Stuart, his son by the Catholic princess Mary of Modena, as heir. James II fled to France after being deposed by William of Orange in 1688, but this did not stop his son, the so-called 'Old Pretender', from conferring the title on his own second son Henry Benedict.[9]

In his twenties, this Duke of York (according to the Jacobite Peerage) served briefly in the French army, but following the disastrous attempt by his elder brother Charles ('Bonnie Prince Charlie' or 'The Young Pretender') to reclaim the English throne, Henry grew convinced that his true calling lay within the Church. In 1747 he became a cardinal, and after a brief, unsuccessful attempt to be recognised as King Henry IX of England in place of George III, contented himself with his spiritual vocation; rather than 'Grand Old Duke' he was thereafter known as the Cardinal Duke of York.

Meanwhile, the Dukedom of York and Albany had been created, the title being held for the first time by Ernest Augustus, the Prince-Bishop of Osnabrück and youngest brother of King George I. After an upbringing in the courts of Europe, Prince Ernest undertook military service, fighting with William III's allied army against the French in the Nine Years' War, where he saw action in the Battle of Landen, or Neerwinden, in 1693. However, he was not created Duke of York and Albany (and Earl of Ulster) until 1716, two years after his brother became king. Thereafter he pursued a diplomatic and political rather than military career, remaining in Germany as the senior representative of the British royal family until he died a childless bachelor in 1728, whereupon his peerages became extinct.[10]

The second Duke of York and Albany was Prince Edward Augustus, younger brother of the future George III. Edward joined the navy as a volunteer in 1758 and was involved in action against the French, including an unauthorised and unsuccessful attack on St Malo, prior to his creation as Duke of York in 1760. Following his brother's accession the same year, Prince Edward became heir presumptive; in 1761 he was promoted from post-captain to rear-admiral, but his proximity to the throne prevented him from continuing in active naval service. The rest of his career seems to have been spent largely in pleasure-seeking, until he fell ill while touring Europe in 1767 and died in Monaco, unmarried and childless, at the age of 28.[11] Grand, yes; old, no; and his brief military career was spent sailing ships back and forth rather than marching men up and down.

A more convincing candidate for the dubious honorific is the third Duke of York and Albany, Prince Frederick Augustus Hanover, second son of King George III. Married to Princess Frederica Charlotte of Prussia, he was conspicuously grand both in appearance – his portraits and statues represent him as a corpulent, heavily bejewelled and decorated figure – and in behaviour, having reputedly drunk and gambled his way through the then gigantic sum of £40,000 in a single year. He was also scandalously connected with a certain Mary Anne Clarke, who alleged that she had sold commissions to would-be army officers during her time as his mistress.[12]

Conceivably, the nursery rhyme refers to his largely unsuccessful campaigns in Flanders in 1793 – 94, as part of an alliance led by Britain and Austria with the objective of invading France and defeating its Revolutionary army. Although Prince Frederick enjoyed some initial success at the Battle of Beaumont in April 1794, due to poor troop deployments and poor co-ordination between the allied commanders he was heavily defeated at Tourcoing and Boxtel, and obliged to withdraw in the spring of 1795 having lost 20,000 men in two years. Notwithstanding these failures, he was appointed Field Marshal in 1795 and Commander-in-Chief of the British forces in 1798. In 1799, he led a force of 30,000 on an expedition to overthrow French control in Holland, but once again, poor communications and battle plans led to defeats at Bergen and Castricum, and another ignominious withdrawal under the Convention of Alkmaar.

It has been suggested that the 'hill' in the rhyme may be the town of Cassel in Flanders, which stands at an elevation of 176 metres above the otherwise flat landscape; the second half of the verse may refer to any of the numerous advances and retreats made by York's forces in the Flanders and Holland campaigns, or to the incompetent and vacillating actions of the allied commanders in general. However, the nearest this duke ever got to Mount Cassel was over ten miles away.[13] He was not 'old', being only in his thirties at the time of these abortive campaigns (whose lack of success cannot be laid entirely at his door), and aged 64 when he died in 1827; nor did he have 'ten thousand men', but at least twice that number. So the nursery rhyme is no more accurate as a reflection of Prince Frederick's military career than it is of Richard Plantagenet's – although the verse is rather more suggestive of 18th century than 15th century origins.

Frederick Augustus is probably the last serious candidate to be the subject of the rhyme. Subsequent Dukes of York - Prince George, later George V (1910 – 1936), and Prince Albert, later George VI (1936 – 1952) are remembered as monarchs rather than dukes, and can be discounted as too recent.

To summarise: as members of the royal family, any and all of the Dukes of York might be called 'grand'; and some of them, including Duke Richard, were demonstrably 'brave' as in the rhyme's other common variant. Of the more feasible subjects, the oldest, in the sense of being the original, is Edmund of Langley – a reputedly ineffective commander, to boot – while Richard Plantagenet was also 'of olden days', and the oldest in years at the time of the campaign that led to his death. James Stuart (King James II) must have marched thousands of men up and down hills many times during his career as an active soldier and grand young duke; Frederick Augustus marched tens of thousands through the Low Countries and suffered humiliations both on the battlefield and in the bedroom. Conceivably, the rhyme may refer to any of them; equally, it fits none exactly, although given his widely publicised major defeats and scandalous private life, Frederick Augustus is perhaps the likeliest target.

Alternatively, it may be a generic rhyme based on the tendency of Dukes of York to pursue military careers and suffer the attendant failures and defeats: for example, Edmund of Langley at Castile; Richard Plantagenet at Wakefield; James Stuart at Dunkirk; Ernest Augustus at Landen; Prince Edward at St Malo; and Frederick Augustus in Flanders and Holland.

A final possibility is that it does not refer to *any* Duke of York, or indeed to any actual personage; it is mere nonsense, a simple lyric for children to sing.[14] But whatever its original source and intention, there is a far more fitting tribute to Richard of York than the title 'Grand Old Duke' - the 15th century epitaph composed for his tomb at Fotheringhay by 'Chester the Herald':

May all noble hearts remember that here lies the flower of gentility, the mighty Duke of York, Richard was his name, a royal prince, a warrior of renown, wise, valiant, of virtuous life, who loved loyalty without malice. Proved the rightful inheritor of the crowns of England and France in many lands, he was found and acknowledged to be the true heir at the parliament held at Westminster. He was also regent and governor of France, kept Normandy from disaster, crossed the river at Pontoise and put the French king and his dauphin to flight. In Ireland he ruled in such a way that he brought peace to the country. Of England he was long Protector; he loved the people and was their defender. He had a noble line of children - God keep them - the eldest of whom is named Edward, who is true king and conquered his right, by great labour and danger he obtained it. He reigns alone to day, he has fair children - God keep them from harm – and this good king, to prove his virtue, knowing that his father had decided that his body should rest at Fotheringhay, had him nobly buried here. This noble duke died at Wakefield; while he was treating for peace, misfortune overtook him, the year sixty, on the thirtieth of December. He was fifty years old, as people remember. Praying God and his very sweet Lady that his soul may rest in Paradise!

Amen.[15]

Notes

1. According to nursery rhyme specialists Iona & Peter Opie in their preface to *The Oxford Nursery Rhyme Book*, 1965, Oxford University Press.
2. '*Infir taris, inoknonis, inmudellsis, in claynonis, canamaretots?*', Iona & Peter Opie, *The Oxford Dictionary of Nursery Rhymes*, 1951, Oxford University Press.
3. *Ibid*, p. 176.
4. Anthony Tuck, 'Edmund of Langley, First Duke of York', *Oxford Dictionary of National Biography*, Oxford University Press, on-line edition, January 2008.
5. Rosemary Horrox, 'Edward, Second Duke of York', *Oxford Dictionary of National Biography*, Oxford University Press, on-line edition, 2004.
6. Mark A. Kishlansky & John Morrill, 'Charles I', *Oxford Dictionary of National Biography*, Oxford University Press, on-line edition, October 2008.
7. W. A. Speck, 'James II and VII', *Oxford Dictionary of National Biography*, Oxford University Press, on-line edition, October 2008.
8. A. Lytton Sells (ed.), *The Memoirs of James II: his campaigns as Duke of York, 1652 – 1660*, Bloomington, 1962.
9. Edward Gregg, 'James Francis Edward (1688   1766)', *Oxford Dictionary of National Biography*, Oxford University Press, on-line edition, January 2007.
10. Matthew Kilburn, 'Ernest Augustus, Prince, duke of York and Albany (1674 – 1728), *Oxford Dictionary of National Biography*, Oxford University Press, on-line edition, May 2005.

11. Matthew Kilburn, 'Edward Augustus, Prince, duke of York and Albany (1739 – 1767), *Oxford Dictionary of National Biography*, Oxford University Press, on-line edition, 2004.

12. H.M. Stephens, 'Frederick, Prince, duke of York and Albany (1763 – 1827), *Oxford Dictionary of National Biography*, Oxford University Press, on-line edition, October 2007. For a fuller account of the Duke's relations with Mary Clarke, see 'Grand Old Duke: The greatest scandal never told' by Andy McSmith, *The Independent*, on-line edition, January 1, 2009.

13. A vigorous defence of Duke Frederick by Colonel Burne is quoted in Opie, *op cit*, 1951, pp. 442 – 443.

14. As suggested by numerous variations on the theme (*ibid*, p. 443): 'O the mighty King of France (or Duke of York), With his twenty thousand men, He marched them up a very high hill, And he marched them down again (known from Warwickshire in 1892); or 'Oh! The famous Duke of York, He marched his men to war; But none of them got to the battle-field Because it was so far'.

15. Livia Visser-Fuchs, 'The French Narratives and the Epitaph' in Sutton and Visser-Fuchs, *op cit*, p. 29.

AFTERWORD: EXONERATION OR BLAME?

The Wars of the Roses consisted of nearly four decades of civil unrest punctuated by outbreaks of open warfare, which cost medieval England tens of thousands of lives and can have left few people untouched by anxiety, injury or the sorrow of bereavement. They were essentially the product of a family divided by power, its members jealous and fearful of each others' claims – York by pedigree, the Beauforts by personality - on the royal favour. This central rift was complicated and exacerbated by similar violent feuds within and between other magnate families, notably the Percys and Nevilles – quarrels that embroiled ever more supporters until the issues polarised at national level with the Wakefield – Towton campaign.

Could the Battle of Wakefield have been avoided? Under the conditions prevailing at the time, arguably not; there is a certain grim inevitability about the repeated patterns of behaviour that led up to it - and persisted until the Houses of Lancaster and York were finally, forcefully united by Henry Tudor.

In that case, who was responsible? Clearly, the three principal protagonists discussed herein all had a hand in affairs. As monarch, it was for Henry VI to keep his factious, competitive and prideful nobility in check – a difficult task to which this mild, easily-swayed man was unequal. Yet the extent to which King Henry can be blamed for his failings is debatable. His reign was beset by intractable problems from the moment it (nominally) began; he grew up bereft of his father's counsel and model of kingly behaviour; he may have been additionally burdened by a predisposition to mental illness, and unquestionably suffered serious breakdowns in adult life. Nonetheless he possessed many virtues, and inspired enduring loyalty in his followers even in the 1460's when their self-interest might have been better served by submitting to Edward IV. Sadly, Henry's qualities did not include the confidence, decisiveness and shrewd authority that had characterised his predecessor, but it hardly seems fair to blame him for what he could not help - a personality lacking strong leadership attributes, the misfortune of his early accession, and the resulting peculiarities of his upbringing - even though the consequences of this deficiency were so dire. For him to recognise his shortcomings and abdicate in favour of an abler man would have required a degree of self-awareness and humility few people possess, and which would have been inconsistent with the 15th century world-view; God had ordained him to rule and in fairness to Henry VI, we should assume that he did so to the best of his ability.

The same might be said of Margaret of Anjou. She too was thrust into a position of power, and one far greater than this relatively obscure princess might have expected to attain or been adequately prepared for. More naturally dynamic

125

and assertive than Henry, Queen Margaret threw herself into her new role with vigour, ardently espousing her husband's cause, family and favourites while simultaneously endeavouring to serve the interests of the French relatives to whom she owed her position. Her closeness to the King, coupled with his malleable character, enabled her to wield considerable influence over him – an influence that could only grow as Henry's mental health declined in the 1450's. Given the prevailing unrest in the realm and support for the developing Yorkist faction, it is unsurprising that Margaret should have shared the Lancastrian suspicion of Duke Richard, viewing him as a serious threat to the regime; but apart from an element of political naïveté and unfairness to York, her only 'fault' was her indefatigable defence, stalwart to the point of recklessness, of her husband and son's interests (and thereby her own). Margaret's spear-heading of the rebellion against the Act of Accord was undoubtedly a prime cause of the battle, but its terms were so intolerable to her that submission was unthinkable. (We might conjecture that the Act would also have been unthinkable to her bypassed son and that even if the Queen and court party *had* accepted it, armed opposition would have merely been deferred until the Lancastrian Prince of Wales came of age).

The Duke of York himself may be seen as another victim of circumstance. A Yorkist prince by descent from both parents, the inheritor of vast estates and married into the highest nobility, his own claim to the throne was valid and his position always likely to provoke envy, enmity and unease. Not unreasonably, given his pedigree and connections, York expected to enjoy the favour of his sovereign and a pre-eminent position at court; but despite a solid record of service to the crown this was not forthcoming. Other magnates may have been predisposed to dislike and distrust him, damning his achievements with faint praise and construing his actions, whatever York's intentions, in the worst possible light. The King and Queen, exposed to a constant drip of negative propaganda from persons they found more congenial, apparently came to share this jaundiced perspective. An increasingly desperate York could only counter his detractors when he was in the King's presence, but while Henry could be persuaded (temporarily, at least) of his good faith, Queen Margaret and her adherents were more resolute in their dislike – particularly given the Duke's forthright criticism of their policies. As the friction between them increased, York was no more disposed to accept situations he found unfair and unjust than was Margaret of Anjou, especially since the security of his career, family and indeed his very life were at stake. Eventually, the combination of fury, frustration, fear, lack of an acceptable alternative, and the knowledge that he was supported by the commons and Yorkist lords drove the Duke to press his own claim to the crown. The resulting compromise satisfied no-one, failed to resolve England's problems and effectively set the scene for the catastrophe of Wakefield.

Were the beneficiaries of King Henry's favour, like the Beauforts and other household men, any more at fault? Not necessarily; they simply did what they could, or what they could get away with, to further their interests, support their sovereign, or to avenge great wrongs they felt themselves to have suffered (from insults real or imagined, up to and including the death of family and friends). The denigration and destruction (literal or metaphorical) of rivals, jockeying for position and advantage, exploitation of opportunities and patronage - these tendencies were not unique to 15th century nobility but have been manifest throughout human history, and the modern worlds of politics and business are still replete with parallels. We might deplore such behaviour but collectively, we have not evolved beyond it and thus are hardly well-placed to sit in judgement.

Who was right or wrong, who acted nobly or ignobly remains a matter of perspective, although the episode does not redound particularly to the credit of anyone concerned: a king and queen too caught up with personalities, and an aristocracy too avid for advancement, to act impartially or for the country's greater good. It must have been a sickening period to live through, vividly evoked by Polydore Vergil's comment on the 'mutual rehearsal of old injuries, and quarrelous repetition... of faults'. The violent emotions unleashed are easy to imagine; so perhaps rather than apportioning blame, we should try to extend a measure of understanding and compassion to all parties. They were constrained by position, social expectations, nature and personal capabilities to do as they did. No doubt they felt equally justified, convinced of their rectitude and in many cases, prepared to hazard their lives in defence of their cause. More than any individual, we might deem the system itself to be at fault, to be the root cause of the battle and indeed the entire Cousins' War: the system of absolute monarchy whereby the fate of the nation, and of the hapless common folk pressed into waging war on their lords' behalf, hung to such an extent on the character and abilities of a king, on the advisers he chose and the policies he pursued.

So does the sympathetic reappraisal attempted in this book represent a 'true' picture of the causes and course of the Battle of Wakefield – or another addition to the oeuvre of myth and imaginative over-interpretation? Admittedly, the version presented here all hinges on the crucial role of Lord Neville (and to a lesser extent, Andrew Trollope): that one or both did indeed approach the Duke of York under the false colour of friendship with a substantial body of troops, only to fight on the Lancastrian side; and that it was primarily Neville's appearance on the field, deceiving York as to his chances of success, that induced him to leave Sandal Castle.

However, it has the merit of straightforward military practicality, explaining or conveniently bypassing aspects of the traditional accounts which are otherwise puzzling or poorly supported by evidence, and obviating any need for the more complex theories outlined in **Chapter 3**. We know from Edward IV's Act of Attainder that John Neville *did* fight for Lancaster at Wakefield; other sources indicate that prior to the battle he was communicating with both sides, suggesting that his actions were the crux of a deliberate plan that virtually guaranteed the Duke of York's emergence and defeat. We also know that such acts of deception are recognised military strategies, commonplace throughout history and certainly at the time – as are reversals of allegiance, bitter personal or political quarrels and the fatal estrangement of family members. Examples in the run-up to Wakefield include the Earl of Wiltshire abandoning York to hitch himself to the more lucrative Lancastrian bandwagon in 1452 – 53, and the rift between York and his son-in-law Exeter, resulting from the latter's conduct in the Ampthill Castle affair and alliance with the hostile Percys. Later instances are the Duke of Somerset's wavering allegiance following his abortive mission to France in 1461; the Earl of Warwick's rejection of Edward IV and the fluctuating loyalty of George, Duke of Clarence in the late 1460's; the *assumption* of treachery at Barnet, (actually a case of 'friendly fire' resulting from mistaken identity); and the conduct of Lord Stanley at Bosworth in 1485. These are easy acts to condemn; yet they are easy enough to comprehend and empathise with, if we can but put ourselves in medieval shoes and consider the feelings as well as the facts of the times. As in the later English Civil War, these participants faced painfully difficult, dangerous choices in terms of who to support and how to reconcile the often conflicting demands of self-interest, family, God and king, when 'the enemy' might be related to them by blood, marriage - or both.

Select Bibliography

All works used in this publication are fully referenced in the Notes at the end of each chapter. Where possible I have tried to adhere to the following primary sources:

Annales Rerum Anglicarum, in *Letters and Papers Illustrative of the Wars of the English in France*, Vol. 2, Part 2, J. Stevenson (ed.), Rolls Series, 1864; *England Under the Yorkists 1460 - 1485*, I.D. Thornley (ed.), 1920; *Chronicles of the White Rose*, LXXXIII, J.C. Giles (ed.), 1843; College of Arms, MS Arundel 48, folio 170 (recto).

'John Benet's Chronicle for the Years 1400 to 1462', *Camden Miscellany XXIV*, G.L. and M.A. Harriss (eds.), Camden Society, 1972.

Britannia, or a Geographical Description of Great Britain and Ireland, William Camden, 1586, revised by Edmund Gibson, 2nd edition, 1722.

Brut or Chronicles of England, F.W.D. Brie (ed.), 1908.

Calendar of State Papers and Manuscripts existing in the Archives and Collections of Milan, A.B. Hinds (ed.), London, 1913; British History Online, www.british-history.ac.uk.

Crowland Chronicle Continuations 1459 – 1486, N. Pronay and J. Cox (eds.), Richard III and Yorkist History Trust, Allan Sutton Publishing, 1986.

An English Chronicle of the Reigns of Richard II, Henry IV, Henry V and Henry VI, J.S. Davies (ed.), Camden Society, 1856.

Robert Fabyan, *The New Chronicles of England and France*, H. Ellis (ed.), 1811

Great Chronicle of London, A.H. Thomas and I.D. Thornley (eds.), 1938.

'Chronicle of William Gregory, Skinner', in *Historical Collections of a Citizen of London in the Fifteenth Century*, J. Gairdner (ed.), Camden Society, 1876.

Edward Halle, *The Union of the Two Noble Families of Lancaster and* York, 1550 edition, Scolar Press, 1970.

Ingulph's Chronicle of the Abbey of Croyland, H.T. Riley (ed.), London, 1854.

John Leland, 'Itinerary', Yorkshire extracts, *Yorkshire Archaeological Journal*, Vol. 10, 1889.

Letters of Queen Margaret of Anjou and Bishop Beckingham and Others, Written in the Reigns of Henry V and Henry VI, Cecil Monro, (ed.), Camden Society, 1968.

The Paston Letters 1422 - 1509, J. Gairdner (ed.), Archibald Constable & Co., 1900.

Short English Chronicle, *Three Fifteenth Century Chronicles*, J. Gairdner (ed.), Camden Society, 1880.

John Stow, *Annales, or a Generall Chronicle of England*, 1615.

Polydore Vergil, *Three Books of Polydore Vergil's English History*, Sir H. Ellis (ed.), Camden Society, 1844.
Vitellius AXVI, *Chronicles of London*, C.L. Kingsford (ed.), 1905.
Jean de Waurin, *Recuil des Chroniques d'Engleterre*, W. and E. Hardy (eds.), 1891.
Whethamsted's Register, H.T. Riley (ed.), Vol. 1, 1872.

The other publications cited most frequently are:

Boardman, A.W., *The Battle of Towton*, Alan Sutton Publishing Ltd., 1994.
Butler, L., *Sandal Castle, Wakefield: The History and Archaeology of a Medieval Castle*, Wakefield Historical Publications, 1991.
Darbyshire, G.A., *From Knights to Squires: The Gentry & Peerage of Towton*, Volume 1, Freezywater Publications, 2008.
Dockray, K., *Henry VI, Margaret of Anjou and the Wars of the Roses: A Source Book*, Sutton Publishing, 2000.
Dockray, K., *Warrior King: The Life of Henry V*, Tempus Publishing, 2007.
Fiorato, V., Boylston, A. and Knüsel, C. (eds.), *Blood Red Roses: The Archaeology of a Mass Grave from the Battle of Towton AD 1461*, Oxbow Books, 2007.
Griffiths, R.A., *King and Country: England and Wales in the Fifteenth Century*, Hambledon Press, 1991.
Haigh, P.A., *The Battle of Wakefield 1460*, Sutton Publishing Ltd., 1996.
Johnson, P.A., *Duke Richard of York 1411 – 1460*, Oxford University Press, 1991.
Maurer, H.E., *Margaret of Anjou: Queenship and Power in Late Medieval England*, Boydell & Brewer, 2003.
Mayes, P., & Butler, L., *Sandal Castle Excavations 1964 – 1973*, Wakefield Historical Publications, 1983.
Oxford Dictionary of National Biography, Oxford University Press, online edition, www.oxforddnd.com.
Postlethwaite, I., *Richard, Third Duke of York*, Yorkshire Branch of the Richard III Society, 1974.
Wolffe, B., *Henry VI*, Eyre Methuen, 1981.

Further Resources:

An excellent digital reconstruction of Sandal Castle and discussion of the battle can be found on the DVD *Sandal Castle: The Battle of Wakefield 1460 & Building Sandal's Castles* by John L. Fox, www.loyaltybindsme.com.

INDEX